The Metric System–
Measures for All Mankind

FRANK ROSS, Jr.

The Metric System– Measures for All Mankind

ILLUSTRATED BY ROBERT GALSTER

S. G. PHILLIPS   *New York*

LIBRARY OF CONGRESS CATALOGING IN PUBLICATION DATA

Ross, Frank Xavier, 1914–

    The metric system—measures for all mankind.

    Bibliography: p. 128

    SUMMARY: Traces the history of weights and measures emphasizing the metric and British systems and discussing the likelihood of United States' adoption of the metric system.

    1. Metric system—juvenile literature. [1. Weights and measures—History. 2. Metric system] I. title.

QC92.5.R67   389'.152   74-14503

ISBN 0-87599-198-X

*This book is fondly dedicated to
Astelle Atterbury—whose friendship
is immeasurable!*

The author wishes to acknowledge with thanks the permission of the U.S. Bureau of Standards to use various drawings as a basis for several of the illustrations in the text.

Contents

Introduction

Weights and measures have been closely interwoven with man's activities since long before recorded history. They have played a vital role in the development of human societies, especially in such areas as trade and commerce, land division, building construction, and technology.

There is strong evidence that systems of weights and measures originated and developed among the ancient Sumerians and Egyptians before 3000 B.C. The Greeks and Romans used weights and measures developed by the earlier civilizations. But they also made contributions to measurement systems to suit their particular needs. Western Europe, in turn, acquired much of its knowledge about weights and measures through Roman military conquests and trading activities. At the height of the power of the Roman Empire, the Roman system of weights and measures was almost universally used in lands extending from the Atlantic Ocean to the Middle East.

Following the collapse of the Roman Empire and the division of the lands it controlled into numerous independent countries, systems of weights and measures of endless variety sprang up like mushrooms. But the Roman influence on many of the newly created systems persisted and has continued right down to modern times. Even our own present system of weights and measures has units whose values are not far removed from those used by the Romans. For example, our foot length and the foot length commonly used by the Romans differ by less than four-tenths of an inch.

By the mid-nineteenth century two of the more important weights and measures systems ever devised had gained dominance throughout the world. One was the British imperial system of weights and measures, and the other was the metric system. The imperial system was the result of centuries of evolution. The metric system, for the most part, was created during the turmoil of the French Revolution.

For more than a century the two systems of measurements competed for supremacy. At first the advantage was with the British imperial units. But as the superior features of the French metric system — simplicity and uniformity, among others — became appreciated by more and more nations, it gained in popularity and acceptance.

With the coming of the twentieth century the contest was just about over. The metric system was being used by a majority of the countries of the world. The climax of the competition arrived in 1965 when the British chose to abandon their own imperial units of measurements for the metric system.

At this writing there remains only one major nation, the United States, that continues to use a modified arrangement of the British imperial measurements. But even in this country, time is rapidly running out for these very old units of weights and measures. To an increasing degree, metric measures are already being used. And the United States Congress is on the verge of passing legislation that will bring this country into the family of nations using metric measurements exclusively. The move is inevitable.

This book is a survey of the historical background of weights and measures. In particular, it is concerned with the origin and modern refinement of the metric system — one of the foremost intellectual achievements of man.

1

Early History of Weights and Measures

The hunt was ended. It had been a good one. The huge wild ox lay dead on the ground, ready to be divided among the hunters. There was noisy excitement and movement among

Primitive man measured and weighed objects by eye and by hand.

the little band of men as they circled the kill. Here was food for several days. Each man waited eagerly for his share of the meat.

The hunters skilled at cutting up the creature began their work. As chunks of flesh were removed each piece was held up and measured by the cutter's eye. Except for the leader, no man was to receive a bigger share than his neighbor.

Perhaps in some such crude way there began the first system of weights and measures. We do not know for certain. All we can be sure of is that even ancient man must have used some means of weighing and measuring to carry on his daily activities.

At some obscure period in time man evolved from a nomad and hunter to a farmer. He grew crops and raised cattle to feed and clothe himself and his family. He gave up caves for man-made shelters, thus bringing the earliest permanent villages into existence.

As time passed, man's occupations became somewhat more specialized. Now he found it necessary to rely on his neighbors for those things which he did not grow or make. This development led to the practice of trading or exchanging various items.

If trading was to be carried out in a practical, fair way, prehistoric man had to work out some method of measuring quantities. The first measure of all, because it was the simplest, may well have been a man's hand or hands, formed into a cup. This could have served for doling out grain to a neighbor in exchange for a newly made digging stick. Later, the measuring unit may have been a crudely hollowed-out portion of a tree or a gourd. If he lived near the seacoast, a shell may have been used for the same purpose.

Since man was now building his own shelters, he needed to know something about length, width, and height, too. It was logical for man to turn to his own body for these linear measurement units. His finger, his hand, his arm, his foot, and even his height were the easiest and most familiar lengths to use for comparison purposes. They were convenient, too, for wherever he went, a man always had his measuring tools with him. He could even make use of his body movements as tools — his reach, for example, with one or both arms extended, or his stride.

As the society of man advanced through the centuries in knowledge and skills, measuring systems and devices became a good deal more sophisticated. The *cubit* was one of the more common linear measurements used by ancient man, and one of the oldest of which we have written records. Its exact length varied rather widely among different peoples and even within a single nation. However, in all cases it was based on the length of the arm from the elbow to the tip of the middle finger. The word comes from the Latin *cubitum,* meaning "elbow." Numerous clay tablets, the records of ancient man, and also the Bible make frequent references to the cubit.

When commanded to build his ark before the coming of the flood, Noah was given precise measurements to use. The ark was to be 300 cubits long, 50 cubits wide, and 30 cubits high. Even if one considers the cubit to measure 17.58 inches, one of the shorter lengths used in ancient times, Noah's ark still would have been a good-sized boat. It would have measured about 439 feet long, 73 feet wide, and 44 feet high.

The cubit was used as a basis for other measurement units, also. For instance, the distance from the tip of the middle finger of the outstretched hand to the middle of the breast was considered to be twice the length of the cubit, and was called the *ell.* By doubling the ell, that is, by measuring from the tip of one middle finger to the tip of the other with both arms extended, the *fathom* was produced. In our numerical measurement terms, the fathom is equal to six feet. A line divided into fathom units, usually by means of knots, was dropped overboard by seamen to measure the depth of the water through which they were sailing.

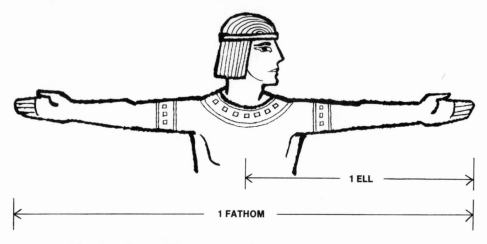

The Greeks and Romans, in later eras, also used the cubit as a length unit, though they preferred the foot as a measure for most of their construction.

The *digit* was another important linear measuring unit used by the peoples of the ancient world. It was based on the width of the finger. Like the cubit, it had a variety of measurements. One of the more popular equaled 0.729 inch in our current system of measures.

Other measuring units based on the hand were the *palm*, about 4 inches, the *great span*, representing the spread between the thumb and the little finger, and the *little span*, which was the greatest possible distance between the tips of the thumb and index finger.

It was certainly convenient to use parts of the human body as linear measurement units, but there were drawbacks. People are just not "standardized." Some are tall and some are short and some are in between, and they have arms and hands and feet of different sizes. As the system of measurements based on the human body became common throughout the ancient world, it produced considerable confusion. Linear dimensions had a name, but the name did not necessarily indicate the same length everywhere. Despite countless attempts to improve the situation, this confusion has continued right up to modern times.

Ancient peoples were aware of the weakness of their

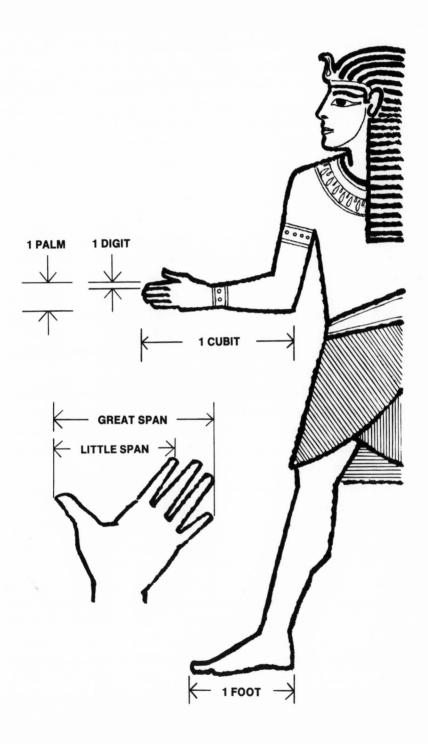

1 PALM

1 DIGIT

1 CUBIT

GREAT SPAN

LITTLE SPAN

1 FOOT

measurement system and they did try to make it more workable by establishing standards. The hand, the arm, and the foot were given uniform measurements that all members of a regional group or a nation agreed to accept, either by common consent or because it was imposed on them by their rulers. Such standardization efforts were fine as far as the people of a single nation were concerned. But they did little to improve measurement standards between people living in different countries. The variations in measurement values continued as before.

At this point it may be in order to say a few words about the terms "units of measure" and "standards." A unit of measure represents the value of a specific quantity of weight or linear or volume measure. Units define the elements that make up a system of measurement. For example, the "pound" is a unit for describing mass (weight); "foot" is a unit describing a measurement of length.

Standards are physical representations of the value of a unit of measure. (The platinum bar once used as the standard for the meter is an example.) They are almost never used for direct measurements. Made with superprecision, standards serve mainly for reference. The everyday units of measurement are checked against standards for accuracy. Where they exist as physical objects, standards are kept in vaults under controlled conditions, such as temperature and humidity.

There is archaeological evidence that efforts to standardize linear measurements were made more than four thousand years ago. The ancient Sumerian city of Lagash was ruled, about 2050 B.C., by King Gudea, who was a great builder. Several statues of King Gudea have been uncovered at the site of this city, and two of them show the king seated with a rule on his lap. The rule is about 10½ inches long. This is believed to represent half the length of one of the longer values given the ancient cubit, that is, 21 inches. The rule on King Gudea's lap also has subdivisions of smaller units. Archaeologists feel that the rule was used in an attempt to standardize the length of the cubit employed by the Sumerians.

Studies of the pyramids of Egypt, built several thousand years ago, indicate that the ancient Egyptians also tried to standardize measurement units. Scholars have concluded that these immense structures could not have been erected so accurately without some system of measurement standards being employed. However, we do not know what the exact standards were.

Up to this point we have been talking exclusively about attempts to standardize linear measurements among the ancient peoples. What about measures of weight and volume? Metrologists (experts in the science of measuring) tell us that this part of measurement systems evolved later. But the development was not too long in coming.

Early civilizations had surprisingly practical systems of weight measurement. Balance scales were in common use in ancient Egypt. We know this from papyri that have survived to this day, and from the paintings on the walls of the tombs of ancient Egyptian kings. And stone weights used as standards have been found in Egypt as well as elsewhere in the Middle East. The oldest weighing device discovered so far is an Egyptian balance with limestone weights that dates from the fifth millennium B.C.

However, the practice of weighing among the ancient peoples was limited for several thousand years, according to metrologists, to determining the weight of gold, silver, gems, and semiprecious minerals. For day-to-day commercial needs where exactness was not required, food and goods were either counted or measured by volume. Volume is the amount of space occupied by a particular substance. It is measured by cubic units, such as cubic inches or cubic centimeters.

Two interesting developments grew out of ancient peoples' restricted use of weight measurements. Their application to precious and semiprecious items led, first, to devising measuring units of amazing exactness. Second, it led to the combining of weight units with money values. The first coins, invented by the Lydians in the seventh century B.C., were disks of precious metal stamped with a special mark to show their weight and purity. It is no accident that the British pound (unit of money) had the same name as the British measure of weight.

Scholars in the field of metrology have traced what many believe to be the earliest precise system of weights and measures to the Middle East. It was the work of the Sumerians, an ancient people who lived in a region between the Tigris and Euphrates rivers, and who developed a remarkably advanced civilization several thousand years before the birth of Christ.

The Sumerians were excellent mathematicians, scientists (astronomers), technologists, and farmers. They built some of the earliest cities in the world. In almost all of these they erected huge, pyramid-shaped temples. The Sumerians also constructed an extensive and effective irrigation system for their farming activities and for controlling floods. They could not have done any of this without a sound understanding of mathematics and a workable system of measurements.

With respect to mathematics, the Sumerians devised a highly ingenious system of numbers. It was partly decimal in nature, that is, based on the number ten, and partly sexagesimal, based on the number sixty. Some of their sexagesimal units are still in use today. The circle, for example, is divided into 360 degrees, and angular measurements are also done on a sexagesimal basis.

It was largely through their skill with numbers that the Sumerians were able to devise a measurement system of an extremely high order, one in which the palm and the cubit were their basic linear units. From clay tablets, the written records of their society that have come down to us, we know that the *palm* measured roughly 3.9 inches. The Sumerian cubit was approximately 5 palms long, or 19.5 inches. Where a longer dimension was needed, Sumerians used a double cubit of 39.0 inches.

Ancient coins, as in these examples, had special marks to show the weight and purity of the precious metals from which they were made.

Ancient Sumerians used a surprisingly advanced system of measuring for constructing their public buildings.

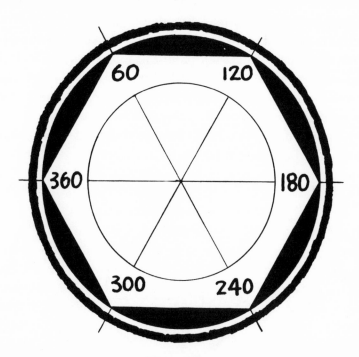

Today's compass card reflects the sexagesimal system of numbers (based on the number sixty) devised by the ancient Sumerians.

The principal Sumerian unit of weight was based on a cube each of whose sides was equal to the length of the palm (3.9 inches). When filled with water the cube produced the unit of weight, the *mina*. The mina was then divided by the Sumerians into smaller units, called *shekels*. Although there was no set standard for the number of shekels to a mina, it was common for 60 of these to make a mina. Since we know that a cubic foot of water (1,728 cubic inches) weighs 62.4 pounds, we can deduce that the mina (3.9 x 3.9 x 3.9 cubic inches) weighed a little over 2 pounds.

Sumerians also used a larger weight unit known as the *talent*, consisting of 60 minas. Note the use of 60 to 1 ratios, related to the sexagesimal or "60" number system, between the shekel, mina, and talent, which became in time the basic coinage and weight measures throughout the Near East. Later, when the Greeks and Romans became supreme in the Mediterranean region, they adopted the Sumerian units.

There is evidence that the Sumerians also made use of scales and stone weights in their system of measures. Although Sumerian scales have yet to be unearthed, stone weights in the form of ducks and lions have been found by archaeologists. The stones have the figures of the weights they represented carved in their surface. These stone weights were kept in the temples of Sumerian cities under the guardianship of the priests. Then, as now, official measuring standards were considered objects of value that were not to be tampered with.

Stone weight standards were used by many of the peoples of the Mediterranean region.

Farm workers in ancient Egypt are shown weighing and recording a field crop.

If the system of weights and measures was developed to an impressive degree by the Sumerians, it flourished brilliantly among the Egyptians. Like the Sumerians, Egyptians were skilled mathematicians. Mainly because of this talent they created a weights and measures system that was remarkably advanced even compared to some systems in use today. Although Sumerians were familiar with and used the figure 10, the base of the decimal system of numbers, in their calculations and weights and measures, the Egyptians employed 10 for the same purposes on a far larger scale. In so doing, the Egyptians anticipated by several thousand years one of the chief features of the modern metric system. Equally significantly, the Egyptian system of weights and measures was standardized to a high degree. As we noted earlier, without this achievement the Egyptians could not have built their impressive temples and pyramids with the precision they have.

The familiar but varying cubit was common in Egypt. It was basically the length from the tip of the elbow to the tip of the middle finger, as elsewhere. Somewhat unusually, the Egyptians maintained two different lengths of the cubit. The first and oldest, perhaps, was the cubit of 6 palms, used by the people generally and particularly by those engaged in commercial activities. The royal cubit, subdivided into 7 palms, weight unit used was a grain of wheat. Various quantities of government structures, temples, and pyramids.

Although linear measurements were of vital importance to the Egyptians for construction purposes, this was not their only application. Linear measurements were also used to determine land areas and for survey work generally. When the Nile River went through its annual flood cycle, inundating the rich farmlands of the delta region, the floodwaters would wipe out the established land boundaries. After they receded, surveyors had to remeasure the land to form new boundaries. In the course of their work, the surveyors made use of a convenient measuring unit called the *khet*. This was a basic square unit having 100 royal cubits to a side.

The Egyptians, no less than other peoples of the ancient Mediterranean world, conducted a flourishing trade inside their own country as well as with other nations. In order to

Ancient Egyptian surveyors measuring a land area.

carry on this activity properly, a system of weight measures was necessary. The need was particularly important for measuring quantities of precious metals. The standard weight unit used was a grain of wheat. Various quantites of grain were used to establish the multiple units of weight.

The *bequa* is one of the oldest known Egyptian terms of weight measurement. It was employed for several different weights. The standards were made of stone shaped like short cylinders with domed ends. The unit of weight which the stone standard represented was inscribed on the cylinder.

When Egyptians measured quantities with the help of the bequa, they did so with numbers based on the factor 10. A balance scale was used with the stone weight standards. The weighing was generally done to determine quantities of precious metals such as gold, silver, and copper.

The Greeks obtained much of their knowledge of weights and measures from other countries of the Mediterranean world. They were far-ranging seafarers, sometimes engaging in peaceful trade and sometimes seeking military

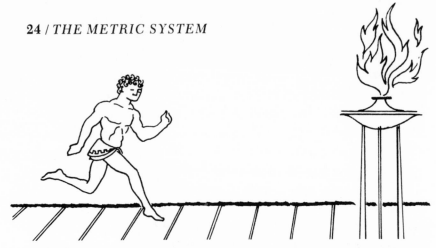

The Greek word *stadion* referred to a length measure of about 600 feet. It became a popular distance run by athletes in the Greek Olympic games.

conquest. When they found linear, weight, and capacity measurements useful to them, they brought the measures home and gave them Greek names.

Among the glories of Greek civilization are what were probably the most beautiful architectural forms ever created by man. In the construction of their marvelously designed temples and public buildings, the Greeks employed the foot as a basic measurement unit more often than the cubit. However, they were familiar with the cubit and did make use of it on a small scale.

The foot, of course, had been derived from human anatomy just as most of the linear measurements were. And because of differences in the dimensions of the human body, the foot length varied. As with other peoples of the ancient world, the Greeks devised a foot unit having more than one value.

The *Attic foot* was commonly used by the Greeks. In our measurement terms, the Attic foot was 12.1375 inches long. This value was derived by historians from measurements taken from the ruins of the Parthenon.

For longer measurements the Greeks employed the *stadion*. Originally, this was the distance a strong man could run while holding his breath. Eventually it stretched to the equivalent of 600 feet in length. This became one of the more popular distances run by athletes in the Greek Olympic games. Incidentally, it is from *stadion* that we obtain our own word "stadium," the home of sports events.

The Grecian system for capacity measurements was a good deal more complicated than that for linear measurements. One of the chief reasons was that the Greeks were a seafaring people who engaged in flourishing trade with other countries of the Mediterranean world. To make matters easier for themselves, and also to reduce the possibility of being cheated, they used the various weight systems of the people with whom they did business.

Later, when their own system of weights became more or less standardized, the Greeks used such units as the *Aegina stater* and the *drachma.*

The Aegina stater (Aegina was the name of a Greek goddess) was based on the shekel. As we described earlier, this was an old and common unit employed throughout the Middle East and Mediterranean regions.

The drachma was established at the beginning of the sixth century B.C. and was based on a fraction of the ancient Sumerian mina. The drachma was used in both a lightweight form, for coinage, and a heavy form, for trading purposes. Weight values were determined by an equivalent weight of a specific number of grains of wheat. The physical weight standard for the drachma was shaped like a dart. (The iron darts used by Greek warriors were called drachmas.)

Some interesting contributions to the development of the language of weights and measures were made by the Romans. They took a great deal of what they needed in this field from the Greeks, whom they conquered. But they obtained many features of their weights and measures system from other peoples as well. The Romans, no less than the Greeks, ranged far from their homeland for military and commercial purposes.

Like the Greeks, the Romans found the foot a convenient measurement unit, but the Roman foot (*pes*) was smaller than that of the Greeks; it was 11.654 inches long.

Actually, the length of the Roman foot was originally based on the Egyptian digit, and was sixteen times the length of the digit. But the Romans divided their foot measure into twelve parts, or *unciae*. This Latin term, meaning "twelfth part," eventually became our "inches." Most of the Roman system of weights and measures was based on a duodecimal numerical arrangement, that is, the use of the number 12 in dividing their standard measuring units. The use of duodecimal values was one of the lasting contributions of the Romans to the development of a system of weights and measures. Even after two thousand years, our present customary system of measurements shows Roman influence. We divide our foot measurement into 12 subdivisions or inches, just as the Romans did.

The Romans used the old linear cubit, too, but to them it had a length of 24 digits. For greater distances there was the famous Roman mile (*milia passuum* in Latin). This came from the extended marches of the Roman soldiers and was equivalent to the ground covered by a thousand two-pace strides, roughly 5,000 feet.

One of the outstanding features of Roman civilization was an excellent system of highways. This gave birth to the popular expression "All roads lead to Rome." At every mile interval along their highways, stone markers were erected for the convenience of travelers, who could tell how far they were from the Roman capital. The markers were also helpful to workmen whose job it was to keep the roads in good repair.

The Romans also made common use of the *iugerum* for measuring land areas. The iugerum was equal to 28,800 square Roman feet. This is about two-thirds of an acre in our measurement system. For weight measurements, the Romans employed among other units a pound measure called the *libra*. This had a value of one-half the weight of the ancient mina. Using the number 12 again, the Romans di-

The amphora was a popular earthenware jar used by ancient Greeks and Romans for measuring, storing, and shipping olive oil and wine.

vided the pound into 12 unciae or ounces. Thus the Latin word *unciae* not only became the word for "inches," but also "ounces." (However, our pound has 16 ounces because of later modifications.)

To measure corn, wheat, and other dry items by volume, the Romans used the *modius* as a basic unit. In modern measurement terms it was equal to about a peck.

For liquid measures the Romans employed a basic unit

called the *sextarius*. This was the equivalent of a modern
pint. Six sextarii (plural of sextarius) made the *congius*, and
eight congii made the *amphora*. (The amphora was also the
name of an earthenware jar commonly used by the Romans
and Greeks for shipping wine and olive oil. Scuba divers
have retrieved many ancient amphorae from the bottom of
the Mediterranean.) The amphora is believed to have been
equal to a cubic foot, Roman measure. Metrologists consider
this an attempt by the Romans to relate measures of capacity
with both mass and linear units in their system of weights
and measures. The value and convenience of this feature of
measurement systems was not to appear significantly again
until centuries later.

Wherever the conquering Roman legions went, they took
with them their system of weights and measures. And since
Roman conquests covered most of the Mediterranean region, along with a good portion of what we today call western
Europe, this meant that Roman units of measurement became almost universally used in the western world. Indeed,
the Roman system of weights and measures was the basis of
the systems that evolved in the western world right up to
modern times.

2

British Weights and Measures

With the breakup of the Roman Empire, many countries and regions went their own independent way. This newfound freedom involved nearly all aspects of their society, including development and use of their own system of weights and measures. As a result, there was a drastic change from what had previously been a nearly universal system of weights and measures to a great number of local and different systems of measures. There evolved systems of weights and measures both within countries and between countries of great variety and confusion. Although many of the new measurement systems represented a clean break from Roman influence, others continued to show in varying degrees a Roman origin.

The complex evolution of weights and measures that took place in Great Britain, in particular, has special significance for us. This is because it is from the British that the United States originally acquired its own system of measurements, although the two systems have developed differences in values.

There was another reason why the British imperial system of measures became important, aside from its

The ancient Anglo-Saxon word tun (tub) gave us our present-day measuring unit ton. In olden times the tun was equivalent to 252 gallons (2,000 pounds) of beer, wine, or other liquid. It was a popular measuring unit used in medieval English breweries.

relation to the United States. The British measurement language was employed throughout much of the world. During the nineteenth century and some of the twentieth, the British ruled a far-flung colonial empire. Not unlike colonizers of other eras, wherever the English established their influence they also introduced their traditions and ways of conducting their affairs. Thus, the British imperial system of measurements and its terminology became about as universal as any that had preceded it.

The British imperial system of measurements had a heritage many centuries old. Exact origins of a number of its measurement terms and the values they represented, dating from the time of the Anglo-Saxons, are unknown. Some came from the period of Roman conquest in 55 B.C. Centuries later, and mostly through trading with the peoples on the continent of Europe, countless new terms and units for weights and linear measures were introduced.

Measurement units for weight and volume during ancient times in England consisted of a particularly long series of confused names and values. One of the oldest of these measurement terms was the *tun*, or tunne, an Anglo-Saxon word for "tub." This term has given us our present-day word "ton." At first, the Anglo-Saxons used the tun for measuring large quantities of various kinds of liquids. Later, the tun was employed for weighing different nonliquid items. Because of its use both for volume and weight measures, the tun, or ton, is an excellent example of how confusing the old English measuring system became.

Over a period of time constant use of the tun made it a standard unit for volume measurements. The large container held 252 gallons of wine, oil, milk, or whatever the Englishmen happened to be dealing with. The tun became a legal unit for measuring liquids.

Eventually the tun and whatever the contents it was to measure became related to the weight unit of 2,000 pounds. This weight is the ton of 20 hundredweight. Unfortunately, in England at the time, the hundredweight was not 100 pounds as the word would imply. Instead, it was 112 pounds. This brought into existence a different ton value of 2,240 pounds.

It was King Henry I who began the confusion over the hundredweight in England. At the beginning the hundredweight was considered to be 100 pounds. But King Henry I did not believe the quantity a true measure of the unit and passed a decree increasing it to 112 pounds. His reason for doing so may have been based on royal household dealings with tradespeople. Perhaps the king felt he ought to get more for his purchases. Although it experienced a subsequent change, the hundredweight of 112 pounds remained in constant use in England up to modern times.

In the world of measurements the British ton of 2,240 pounds became known as the long ton and the American ton of 2,000 pounds as the short ton. The variation presented a convenient opportunity for some in the commercial field to engage in questionable practices. For example, in the coalfields of Pennsylvania, coal miners at one time were paid for their work on the basis of the long ton. But the owners of the coal mines sold this essential product on the basis of a short ton. The unfairness of the arrangement was eventually recognized and the practice outlawed by the federal government.

Although the long and short tons are the two main units of this maximum weight measurement today, they are by no means the only variations of the original volume ton. As special needs arose, other kinds of volume ton units came into existence.

Two that have a very particular meaning in the maritime field are the *register ton* of 100 cubic feet and the *displacement ton* of about 35 cubic feet. The former is used for measuring the interior capacity of ships, the latter for designating the displacement or weight of empty ships. Displacement relates to the amount of water displaced by a ship at anchor. With respect to a ship's weight this amount is determined by calculating the cubic dimensions — length, width, and height — of a ship.

Two other existing forms of the volume ton are the *timber ton*, of 40 cubic feet, and the *wheat ton*, consisting of 20 bushels of grain. Both units are restricted in usage to lumbering and farming activities.

The *pipe* and the *hogshead* were other old terms of the British measurements system used to designate specific volumes. One pipe (no relation to the pipe for smoking) was equal to about ½ ton (British measure) or almost as much by volume as was held by two hogsheads. The pipe was used to measure quantities of beer and whiskey. The hogshead, employed for measuring beer and ale, was the equivalent of 2 barrels in measurement, or roughly 31.5 gallons. The barrel measurement had a number of different values in the old days and it still does today.

In the United States, for example, many of the states have their own ideas about what a barrel should contain by volume. They are especially concerned about this for taxation purposes. While the federal government recognizes a barrel of 31 gallons for taxing liquor, a number of the states fix the barrel for this same purpose at the old British figure of 31.5 gallons. Adding to the confusion, in the petroleum industry it has long been the custom for a barrel of crude oil to consist of 42 gallons. This unit of measure is recognized by only four states, again chiefly for taxation reasons.

The gallon unit of measurement is a good example of the enormously complex, confused nature of English weights and measures during medieval times. The gallon unit for measuring wine was not the same as the gallon unit for measuring an equal quantity of oil or other liquids. And even the gallon unit for wine was not the same in one part of England as it was in another. To make matters worse, the gallon measure was often reckoned on the basis of weight rather than cubic quantity.

To a great degree the confusion in old English measurements was due to the fact that communication between various parts of medieval England was almost nonexistent. An occasional foot traveler or horseback rider bridged the distance between communities, but people born in certain villages or towns, or in rural areas, generally spent their entire lives there and seldom ventured to distant localities. They knew little about their faraway neighbors and probably had even less interest in them.

This absence of community contact led to the development of what amounted to nearly independent and localized weights and measures: measurement units with their own particular names and values. Thus, for weight measures, Englishmen dealt with the *clove, stone*, and *sack* among other units. If capacity measure was wanted, then such units as the *pottle, firkin*, or *cartload* were made use of.

The lack of uniformity in weights and measures throughout medieval England was made more acute by the practice of many trades and occupations which developed separate measurement systems just for their use. For example, English surveyors used *poles* and *chains;* druggists employed *minims* and *drams;* and seamen worked with such measures as *fathoms, knots,* and *cable lengths.*

The complexity and absence of uniformity in the system of weights and measures in old England was clearly recognized by that country's early rulers. From time to time over the centuries, English monarchs made attempts to simplify and standardize the system. Sometimes their efforts proved successful, while at other times they simply made a bad situation worse.

It is said that one of the earliest efforts to bring some order to British measurements was made by King Edgar (ruled 959–975), who is credited with having proclaimed that the yard was to equal the length of the distance from the tip of the nose to the tip of the middle finger with the arm fully extended. This may be history or it may be simply a legend; at any rate it was King Edgar who decreed that "the measures of Winchester shall be the standards."

In the days of the early Anglo-Saxon kings, Winchester served as the country's capital. During the reigns of later English kings, bronze containers representing legal gallons (wine) and bushels were kept at Winchester, as physical measurement standards. Iron copies of these standards were made and distributed to sheriffs and magistrates in different parts of the country.

No significant changes were made in weights and measures following the Norman conquest of England in 1066. However, the Normans did transfer the standards at Winchester to Westminster Abbey in London.

Another early attempt at making England's system of weights and measures more uniform appears in the Magna Carta. King John of England was forced by his barons to sign the Magna Carta, or Great Charter, at Runnymede in 1215. It was one of the earliest documents of the western world to deal with human rights and freedom. The charter guaranteed the nobility certain privileges; there was to be no interference in church affairs by the king; illegal levies by the king were to end; and freemen were to have the right of protection by law. The charter eventually also served as the basis for the right of trial by jury. Along with its references to human freedom, the charter stated that "there should be throughout the realm, one measure of wine, one of ale, and one of corn . . . and that it should be of weights as of measures." C823731 co. schools

The Assize of Bread and Ale signed by King Henry III in 1266 dealt very importantly with English weights and measures. Assize was part of the system of law in old England. It was concerned with the issuance of laws from time to time by a state council in the name of the king. These laws had to do with nearly all features of English society. The Assize of 1266 was an effort to clarify the tower system of weight and capacity units. It decreed, "An English penny, called a sterling, round and without clipping, shall weigh thirty-two wheat corns in the midst of the ear; and twenty pence do make an ounce, and twelve ounces a pound; and eight pounds do make a gallon of wine . . ." The tower referred to was the Tower of London, a royal residence in the Middle Ages.

Jumping to the early decades of the fourteenth century we find English laws establishing standards for specific units of linear measure. The inch was to be three barleycorns, round and dry; the foot, 12 inches; the yard, 3 feet; the perch,

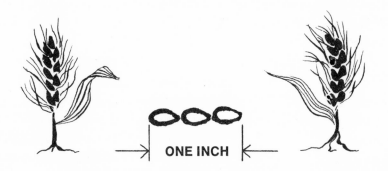

ONE INCH

In fourteenth century England three barleycorns placed end-to-end was the standard for 1 inch.

5½ yards; and the acre, 40 perches long by 4 perches wide.

Changes continued in English weights and measures late in the fifteenth century. King Henry VII issued a law that revised the measurement unit of the gallon. This law was also the first effort to state what quantities the pint and quart should legally contain. According to King Henry's edict, the gallon was to be equivalent to 100 ounces of wheat; the pint to 12½ troy ounces of wheat, and the quart to 25 ounces of wheat. Troy weight was a French unit of which more will be said shortly.

The efforts to clear up the complexities of early English weights and measures just described were really not too successful. The bishop of Fleetwood, writing in the eighteenth century about the confused system of weights and measures existing in England at the time, commented on King Edgar's early effort to standardize measures and the whole situation generally. "It was a good law of King Edgar that there should be the same money, the same weight, and the same measures, throughout the kingdom, but it was never well observed. What can be more vexatious and unprofitable, both to men of reading and practice, than to find when they go out of one country into another, they must learn a new language or cannot buy or sell anything. An acre is not an acre, nor a bushel a bushel if you go from a goldsmith to a grocer, nor a gallon a gallon if you go from the alehouse to the tavern. What purpose does this variety serve, or what necessity is there, which the difference of price would not better answer and supply?"

There was probably no unit in the old English system of weights and measures that was more "English" in origin than the pound. Since the early days of the Saxons it has been used as a unit both for weight and for coinage. In medieval England and later, there were several different pound measures in existence. And these pounds were subdivided in various ways, into ounces, scruples, or grains.

The Tower pound was the earliest and, as we have seen, was defined by the Assize of 1266 as containing 12 ounces.

This scene shows a medieval coin maker at work.

The Tower pound was the legal mint pound, largely restricted for the use of coinage.

There was also a commercial pound used by the people for their everyday needs. It was heavier than the Tower pound by nearly 25 percent, weighing close to 15 ounces. This unit was also in common use on the continent of Europe.

Both the Tower pound and the commercial pound were eventually replaced by two French weight units, the *Troy pound* and the *avoirdupois* pound. The troy measure derives its name from the French city of Troyes, where the pound weight is believed to have originated.

King Henry VIII liked the troy measure so well for the minting of money that in 1527 he abolished the Tower pound that had long been used for this purpose. The troy pound thereafter became the legal standard for coinage.

The avoirdupois pound was the second of the French units of weight to make its appearance in England. It is not known exactly when this took place. *Avoirdupois* is an old medieval French term meaning "goods of weight." It was applied to bulky items, as in the weighing of wool. When brought to England the avoirdupois unit was calculated at 16 ounces to the pound. In time, it took such firm root in England that it has been used as a convenient unit of weight right up to the modern era. It is still a weight unit in the United States.

In England, and other parts of Europe, still another weight unit was employed, the *carat*. The word and the unit came from the Arabs and is based on the weight of the carob seed. The carat was used, and still is, for measuring the weight of diamonds and the fineness of gold.

This drawing shows the comparison in weight of the avoirdupois pound on the left and the troy pound on the right.

At this point an explanation is in order regarding the terms "weight" and "mass." In almost all instances the word "weight" is used when, more accurately, the word "mass" should be employed instead. However, long usage of the word "weight" when we speak of light or heavy objects has made it an inseparable part of our vocabulary. For everyday use of the word, it really does not make much difference. But wherever accuracy is involved, as in science or engineering, then there is a sharp distinction and "mass" must be employed.

When we speak of the weight of an object, we actually mean its mass. Weight is related to the force of gravity pulling upon an object. Thus an object light in mass will be influenced lightly by the pull of gravity and is therefore of light weight. An object of heavier mass will be influenced more strongly by the force of gravity and is therefore said to be of heavy weight.

If we were aboard the Skylab, circling many miles above the earth, and released our hold of a Ping-Pong ball, it would float about within the cabin. The ball has the same mass on Skylab that it has on earth, but it has practically no weight because of the very slight effect of gravity.

On earth the Ping-Pong ball would drop right to the ground. Its mass would represent a much larger weight because of the stronger pull of gravity.

For convenience, reference will be made to weight in the pages ahead although mass is really the factor involved.

Almost as much confusion surrounded early British linear measurements as existed with weight and volume units. When the Romans came and conquered the inhabitants, they brought all the trappings of their civilization, including a system of weights and measures. The Roman foot, for example, was employed by the Romans for building purposes; as mentioned earlier, it was about 11.65 of our inches.

Soon after the Romans left the British Isles in the fifth century A.D., the Angles and Saxons came in successive invasions from northern Europe. They brought with them their own linear units. One was the *Drusian foot*, having a length of 13.2 inches. Another was a foot measure that, as legend has it, was based on the length of Emperor Charlemagne's foot.

By the early fourteenth century the English had a considerable number of different foot lengths to choose from. King Edward I was the ruler at this time and he decided that there had to be some clarification of this most important unit of linear measure. It was this monarch, as we noted earlier, who declared that the inch was to equal 3 barleycorns (kernels) taken from the center of the ear and placed end-to-end. The foot was to be the equivalent of 36 barleycorns, also to be taken from the center of the ear and placed end-to-end. This came very close to the 12-inch foot we know today.

We are all familiar with the linear *yard*. In earliest times in Britain the measurement unit for yard was referred to as the *gird* or girth. According to legend, the gird came from the length of a belt worn by Saxon kings. When necessary, this belt could be conveniently removed and used as a measuring device.

In the reign of King Henry I (1100–1135) the legal yard measurement was made the length of the monarch's arm. Eventually the measurement unit changed again, and was considered the length from a person's nose to the tip of his middle finger with the arm fully extended. Actually, this was a revival of the ell, the linear unit familiar to the ancient peoples of the Mediterranean region. The technique is still often used for measuring the approximate length of a yard by anyone buying fabric.

The *rod* was an equally common measurement term in medieval England. In those days it was spelled "rodd" and referred to a thin branch cut from a tree. It also came to mean a cane and subsequently, in the system of measurements, a stick for measuring a specific length. After numerous variations the rod now designates a linear measurement of 16½ feet.

An ancient Anglo-Saxon term still employed in the field of measurements is the *furlong*. It comes from two words, "furrow" and "long." The furrow, a term well known to farmers, refers to the long depression cut in the soil by a plow. The length of the furrow (or furrow-long) had importance to the farmer of old for it marked the boundaries of the area to be plowed.

As far as can be determined, it seems that the length of a furrow, or furlong, was always in the neighborhood of 660 feet (220 yards) — exactly what it represents today. The word

The linear yard, often referred to as *gird* or girth in medieval England, came, according to legend, from the length of a belt worn by Saxon kings.

"furlong," however, no longer has meaning to the farmer. Now it is a common term in horse racing, indicating a division in the length of a race to be run. A race of 6 furlongs, for example, is ¾ of a mile, since 8 furlongs equal 1 mile.

The *mile* is another British linear measure that is old in history. The Roman 5,000-foot mile was accepted and widely used in Great Britain, even long after the Romans left. Eventually, however, it was found to be awkward; it was impossible to divide the English standard for the furlong, 220 yards, into the Roman mile without producing confusing fractions.

In the sixteenth century, Queen Elizabeth I solved the problem by declaring that henceforth the mile was to measure 5,280 feet — exactly 8 furlongs, since the furlong was 660 feet. Wherever the English system of weights and measures was adopted, this unit became the standard statute mile, or land mile.

The phrase "land mile" is used to distinguish it from the *nautical mile*. Mariners, who had to make elaborate navigational calculations at sea, wanted a mile related, not to the furlong, but to the compass, on which a sixtieth of a degree, or 1 minute, equals a nautical mile of 6,080 feet. This was worked out early in the eighteenth century. The nautical mile was used for many years by seamen of Great Britain, the United States, and other maritime countries.

In 1929 American mariners proposed a new and more precise nautical mile of 6,076.1 feet, based on the latest scientific measurements of the earth's circumference. Nothing much was done about the proposal until 1954, after which most of the maritime nations adopted the new nautical mile, now referred to as the *international nautical mile*.

The task of trying to bring order out of the chaos of British weights and measures has continued up to modern times. A great many additional laws were passed and decrees issued in attempts to simplify and standardize the various measures. By the late nineteenth century the British language of weights and measures had become more or less stabilized, and was commonly referred to as the British imperial system.

As pointed out earlier, this British system of measures was employed in many parts of the world for long periods. Because of its extensive refinement, there was nothing drastically wrong with it. On the whole, people felt that even with the imperial system's somewhat complicated nature, it was working well.

However, in the mid-1960s the British government decided to replace the imperial system of measures with the metric system. By 1965 almost the whole world was weighing and measuring with metric units. For economic reasons, among others, British government leaders felt it was necessary to join those countries using metric measures.

Countries that had already adopted the metric system preferred to trade with countries having the same kinds of weights and measures. For one thing, it was a lot easier to obtain and use spare parts for machines and other industrial equipment made to metric dimensions. If British manufacturers were to be able to sell their products to metric countries, then they would have to make these products according to metric units of weight and measure.

3

Birth of the Metric System

Throughout the Middle Ages and up until the late eighteenth century, England's hodgepodge system of weights and measures had many counterparts on the mainland of Europe. Varying systems of measurements were used in the many countries, and also in regions of the same country. A student of metrology once recorded more than 280 values of the foot among European nations that were used well into the nineteenth century.

Before the Middle Ages and even during them the lack of a uniform system of weights and measures in Europe did not cause too many serious problems. Most of the inhabitants of the various countries lived their whole lives in one locality and were engaged in very simple occupations. Their needs as far as measurements of the foot, pound, or gallon were concerned were taken care of well enough by whatever system of weights and measures had evolved in their midst through common local usage. Parts of the human body — foot, arm, or hand — and man-made or natural objects were the common bases of these units.

In later times, however, and especially during the decades following the industrial revolution, conditions among different societies changed, sometimes drastically.

For example, there arose a vigorous desire to conduct trade both within and outside the bounds of a country.

As efforts to trade increased, an unexpected difficulty became more and more obvious. Even though a pound was called a pound — how much did it weigh? Not only was there a difference between France and Germany, but two towns a hundred miles apart in either of these countries might not agree. A foot in one village could well be a half inch shorter than a foot in a village a day's journey away — or nearly an inch longer. Much the same held true for the gallon, the bushel, and other measures.

The lack of common measurement standards slowed the interchange of goods. Traders were increasingly frustrated. Eventually they became a strong force in the campaign for a simpler and more universal system of measures between nations.

Late in the eighteenth century another development contributed importantly to the feeling that a new system of weights and measures was needed. This was the rise in activity in science and technology.

For many centuries following the downfall of the Greek and Roman civilizations, scientists and their work had been looked upon with disfavor. The church and many government leaders frowned on intellectual activity. It was feared that new knowledge would weaken people's faith in the beliefs of the church, or their support for a ruling king. To discourage such activity, torture and death often awaited those who dared to question established beliefs or to present new ideas.

With the coming of the Renaissance, an age that witnessed a rebirth in and an appreciation for intellectual activity, the scientist's position in society started to improve.

As the scientists flourished and greatly increased the range and quantity of their work, they found that their efforts in many instances were being seriously hampered by an inconsistent and unstandardized system of weights and

Scientists of the Middle Ages are shown using a simple measuring device.

measures. Their researches in such fields as chemistry, physics, and medicine required measurements that were more precise and uniform than those then in existence. Also, scientists like Newton and Lavoisier wanted and needed to exchange their ideas and findings with colleagues of other nations. It was difficult to do this without a common language of measures.

Much the same situation existed among the engineers and technologists, whose job it was to convert many of the theoretical findings of the scientists into practical realities. Watt invented the steam engine, but engineers and technicians built them. And the most serious problem they had to contend with was the lack of uniformity in measurement standards.

Because they shared a common difficulty, scientists and engineers raised their voices as one to urge the establishment of a better system of weights and measures. Other educated groups, including teachers and some clergymen, later joined in this movement.

During the seventeenth and eighteenth centuries, France was one of Europe's leading centers of intellectual activity. It was quite natural therefore that one of the earliest and major efforts to create a new system of measures should take place there. In 1670, Gabriel Mouton, vicar of St. Paul's Church, Lyons, and a scholar, made a proposal for a new system of weights and measures based on decimal units. He submitted his ideas on the subject to the members of the French Academy of Science in Paris.

Vicar Mouton proposed that the basic unit for his new system of measures be taken from the physical universe instead of from the human body. His base unit of length would be the length of an arc of 1 minute of a great circle of the earth (a full line of longitude or latitude). This is 1/60 degree; in turn, there are 360 degrees in a great circle. The vicar called this unit the *milliare*. He further divided the base unit by successive powers of 10 to get subunits. Mouton chose one unit that corresponded roughly to the French foot then in common use.

The members of the French Academy of Science received Vicar Mouton's proposal with only mild interest. They could see no particular reason for changing the language of measures at that time, especially since there were many other more important scientific matters to be considered. Mouton's plan was placed in the academy's archives where it lay for more than a century, until more favorable conditions arose for it to attract attention.

Although Gabriel Mouton is considered a pioneer among those advancing ideas for new decimal systems of measurements, he was not actually the first. In 1585, Simon Stevin, a Flemish mathematician, had suggested a decimal arrangement of measures to replace the complex system then used. Like Mouton's plan, the Dutchman's proposal had aroused little interest and was soon forgotten.

In the last half of the eighteenth century, the western world was rocked by political and social upheaval. In America a new nation, the United States, was born; in France a government of kings was overthrown and replaced by a republic. It was in this climate of revolution and change that the idea of a metric system of measures took root and flourished.

Charles-Maurice Talleyrand was a brilliant government leader who emerged from the turmoil of the French Revolution. One day in April 1790 he addressed the revolutionary National Assembly. To the surprise of the members present, his topic was not political, as expected; it dealt with a plan to reform France's system of weights and measures. Talleyrand had given the subject considerable study and made several concrete proposals.

It was Talleyrand's belief that whatever new system might be adopted, the basic unit of linear measurement should be based on the length of a pendulum. The pendulum device had to operate at the latitude of 45 degrees, that is, halfway from the equator to the north pole. To find the exact length of a pendulum with 1-second arc, scientists would have to carry out new and extremely accurate measurements. This would be a task for the French Academy, an organization of distinguished scientists.

Finally, Talleyrand told his assembled colleagues that if a new system of measures was created, it ought to be of such a nature that more than one nation could adopt and use it. It was his hope that the new language of measures would be universal.

The members of the National Assembly approved Talleyrand's suggestion with a decree, May 8, 1790, directing the French Academy to begin a study of the subject. In keeping with Talleyrand's idea of making the new language of measures a universal one, if possible, the revolutionary National Assembly invited scientists of the Royal Academy of England to collaborate with their French counterparts.

The French Academy appointed several committees to begin the study for a new system of weights and measures. The committees consisted of some of the most distinguished scientists in France. Among them was Antoine Laurent Lavoisier, who, because of his notable achievements, especially the discovery of oxygen, is sometimes referred to today as the founder of the science of chemistry. The conference began without the British, who had ignored the invitation to participate in the discussions.

One committee made a quick report on October 27, 1790. Its members had the rather easy task of deciding that it would be best to adopt the decimal basis for the new measurements system. But the major work of the study — defining and choosing a new basic unit of length measurement — was more difficult. The committee working on this phase of the subject did not make its decision known until March 19, 1791.

What could be used as a basic standard for the new system? Certainly it must no longer be anything so imprecise as a hand or foot; it must have a scientific definition and origin.

It was on this last point that the discussions of the committee members grew very heated. Each of the scientists had strong opinions on the proposals considered.

The committee finally narrowed its discussion on a basic unit of length to three possibilities. One involved the idea proposed by Talleyrand: the precise length of a pendulum that would take exactly 1 second to swing from one end of its arc to the other. (Note: The length of a pendulum determines the time of the swing.) A second was to base the standard on a portion of the length of a circle around the earth at the equator (latitude). The third proposal was similar to the second, except that the section of the earth's meridian to be measured was to extend between the north pole and the equator (longitude). The third proposal won out in the end; the committee recommended that the base unit of length be equal to one ten-millionth of the length of a quadrant of the earth's meridian (one ten-millionth of an arc representing the distance between the north pole and the equator). The *quadrant*, a Latin term denoting one-quarter, is a segment of a complete circle girdling the earth.

It was further recommended by the committee that the portion of the arc of meridian to be measured should be between Dunkirk, in northern France, and Barcelona on the Mediterranean coast of Spain.

The arc of meridian between Dunkirk and Barcelona was selected specifically because the land areas involved had been surveyed years earlier. The mathematical data from the early survey made it possible to work out a temporary length standard until completion of a more accurate survey.

The work of the committee included other phases of creating a new system of measures. The unit of weight for the new system was to be obtained by cubing some part of the unit for the length standard and filling the cube with water. The same method would provide a capacity measure. As a result, the standards of length, mass, and capacity could all be gotten from one linear measurement. Because of their

natural origins these standards could be reproduced end-
lessly and precisely. The use of decimals for multiples and
subdivisions would make the new system extremely convenient.

After the various committees of the Academy had sent
their reports to the National Assembly, the recommendations
for a new system of measures were not immediately acted
upon. Assembly members were solely occupied with political matters, the revolt of French people against their government, which reached an explosive climax in 1793.

They blamed the king for their being oppressed and held

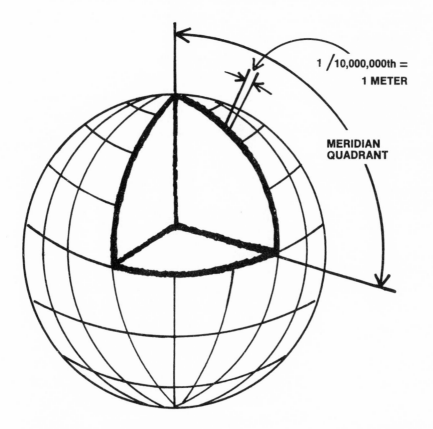

1 /10,000,000th =
1 METER

MERIDIAN
QUADRANT

The original standard for the meter was based on one ten-millionth of the length of
a meridian quadrant.

in extreme poverty. After reaching the end of their patience over empty promises, they angrily took to the streets, killing and destroying anyone and everything having to do with the hated monarchy. Mob rule brought on a reign of terror. The guillotine was in daily operation. This was the favorite execution device of the French. It worked by means of a heavy steel knife which plunged from the top of a scaffold and cut off the victim's head.

The revolution did not spare the members of the Academy. They were scattered and some were even sent to the guillotine, like Lavoisier.

But the leaders of the revolution were determined to break with the past in all aspects of their society. For this reason the idea for a new system of measures was looked upon with favor and even carried forward to completion. Other scientists were given the task of working out the details for a new system recommended by previous Academy members. Survey teams led by the astronomers Mechain and Delambre were sent into the field to survey the arc of the meridian between Dunkirk and Barcelona.

In 1793 those involved with the creation of a new French system of measures decided to name the new length standard the *mètre*, or "measure." The word was from the Greek term *metron*, also meaning "measure." Our English version of the word is *meter*. Because of its basic function in the new system of measurements, the word was also chosen to identify the new system of measurement as the *metric system*.

As proposed several years earlier, the numerical values of the metric system were to be in decimal relation, increasing and decreasing by factors of 10. The scientists had decided with the full agreement of the lawmakers that this arrangement would make for a simple, easy means of converting values of the system from one to another.

Careful thought was given to other features of the metric system, such as the names by which the numerical units were to be known. Some scientists felt that if a few of the names of the old system were used, the general public would accept the new system more easily. But the majority believed that, since the whole system of measures was new, its units should have new names too, and this opinion prevailed in the end.

The creators of the metric system decided to identify the numerical values by using Greek and Latin prefixes. Greek prefixes would indicate multiples of the units; Latin prefixes would denote submultiples. The Greek prefixes chosen for multiples were: *myria* = 10,000; *kilo* = 1,000; *hecto* = 100; *deca* = 10; and no prefix, 1. The Latin prefixes chosen as submultiples were: *deci* = 1/10; *centi* = 1/100; and *milli* = 1/1,000.

The first arrangement of the linear metric system had this appearance:

myriameter	10,000 meters
kilometer	1,000 meters
hectometer	100 meters
decameter	10 meters
meter	1 meter
decimeter	0.1 meter
centimeter	0.01 meter
millimeter	0.001 meter

The weight standard of the metric measure was to be based on the *gram* (also spelled "gramme," especially in the United Kingdom). This was defined as the absolute (limit of scientific testing) weight of a volume of pure water equal to a cube of one-hundredth part of a meter, that is, a cubic centimeter, at the temperature of melting ice. For the weight measures of the metric system the same prefixes were used for the multiples and submultiples of the various units. This is a feature of the metric system that makes for great simplicity and uniformity.

The arrangement of the weight metric system was like this:

myriagram	10,000 grams
kilogram	1,000 grams
hectogram	100 grams
decagram	10 grams
gram	1 gram
decigram	0.1 gram
centigram	0.01 gram
milligram	0.001 gram

The liter was to be used for measuring volume of both liquid and dry materials. It was defined as the equivalent of a cube of 1/10 meter on a side. Prefixes for the liter, with its multiples and submultiples, were:

myrialiter	10,000 liters
kiloliter	1,000 liters
hectoliter	100 liters
decaliter	10 liters
liter	1 liter
deciliter	0.1 liter
centiliter	0.01 liter
milliliter	0.001 liter

In addition to the major provisions of the original metric system, its creators included several special measures. One was the *are*, used to designate the measure of area for land. It was equal to a square 10 meters on a side. The centiare, or one-hundredth of an are, was equivalent to 1 square meter; the hectare, or 100 ares, was equivalent to 10,000 square meters. Another special measure was the *stere*, designated especially for firewood and equal to a cubic meter.

The scientists who helped create the metric system, as well as most of the lawmakers of the French National Assembly who evaluated their achievement, felt that the new system of measures was a big improvement over the old measures. The metric system had simplicity and logical arrangement, mostly because of a close interrelationship of its major parts. In order to use the metric system it was necessary to know only these three features:

1. Its three basic units: the meter, the liter, and the gram.
2. The method of multiplying or dividing these basic units by the power of 10 (the decimal system).
3. The uniform set of prefixes for designating the multiples and the subdivisions.

For example, when the meter is divided by 10 (deci-) it becomes the decimeter; divided by 100 (centi-), the centimeter; by 1,000 (milli-), the millimeter. Going to larger values, when the meter is multiplied by 1,000 (kilo-), the kilometer is formed, and so on.

In 1795, with the reign of terror over, the French National Assembly passed a law making the metric system the legal language of weights and measures in France. Still influenced by the spirit of revolution that continued to envelop France, the law was officially known as the Measures of the Republic. The law made clear that the provisional standard for the new system was to be the meter (*mètre*), based on the length equal to one ten-millionth part of the meridian, or quadrant, between the north pole and the equator. The provisional meter was to remain in force until the survey work of Mechain and Delambre was completed. From the data they acquired, a permanent and more precise basic meter unit was to be computed.

Surveying is a science that applies mathematics for determining exactly points and directions on the earth's surface. Some land features surveyors measure include boundaries, areas, and elevations. To obtain their information surveyors must first measure and then determine results through mathematical calculations. The mathematics used is based

Eighteenth-century surveyors are shown at work. The chain was one of their most important tools for determining lengths.

largely on the principles of geometry and trigonometry. The final data are often transferred to maps or plans.

For making direct measurements surveyors use such tools as the surveyor's chain. This consists of 100 links and is 66 feet long. A similar tool is the engineer's chain, also of 100 links but 100 feet in length. Today, both tools have been largely replaced by the steel tape measure.

In order to find the height of elevated points, surveyors employ a telescope mounted on a tripod. This has a spirit level to help the surveyors keep the telescope in a straight position, especially on rough ground.

Surveyors use still another kind of adjustable telescope called a transit, or transit theodolite, for measuring vertical and horizontal angles.

Survey work is generally not the easiest of occupations, especially when surveyors must perform their tedious activities over a distance of hundreds of miles and across extremely varied terrain. Rain, snow, cold, or fog can add enormously to the difficulties of carrying and using their equipment. Bad weather conditions can be a very serious problem if the surveyors are working to a definite schedule. To succeed in the face of countless obstacles, surveyors must have physical stamina and much patience.

Aside from these basic requirements, it turned out that the French survey parties sent into the field to gather data for the meter standard needed an unusual additional talent — they had to be skilled diplomats. The people of many of the areas in which they surveyed looked upon them with considerable suspicion. They did not understand the purpose of the intruders and hindered them in every way possible. Indeed, in some instances local authorities put the men in jail until they were satisfied that the surveyors were actually on legitimate government business.

The public hostility met with by the surveyors could be explained by the fact that France in the late eighteenth and early nineteenth century was just recovering from the angriest and bloodiest phases of the revolution. There was an atmosphere of strong distrust among the people, not only toward one another but also, and particularly, toward the government and its representatives. With these difficulties, presented to the survey teams by the French people, added to the natural problems that faced them, it was hardly surprising that they required almost six years to complete their task, in November 1798.

The mathematical data gathered by the surveyors was used by scientists to compute a precise standard for the meter. At the end of their calculations they produced a standard length of 39.37008 inches, expressed in the present American system of measurements. Even the most primitive measurement system needs a physical representative for the standard unit; the French scientists decided to use a platinum bar as the physical replica of the meter. Platinum was chosen because it was very stable under a variety of conditions, such as heat and cold, and resisted corrosion.

After the platinum meter bar was made, the French scientists needed a physical standard for the basic unit of weight, or mass, called the gram, and equal to the weight of a cubic centimeter of water. To represent this accurately as a physical quantity was a problem. The unit would have been too small.

Instead, the scientists thought it would be more practical to have, as a physical standard, the kilogram, or 1,000 grams. Consequently, they had made a cylinder of platinum weighing exactly as much as 1,000 cubic centimeters of pure water at the temperature of melting ice. Converting this to the present American equivalent measure, it was equal to 2.2046 pounds.

The liter, the basic volume unit, did not require a physical standard since it was derived directly from the meter, according to its legal definition. The liter is 1,000 cubic centimeters, or $10 \times 10 \times 10$ cm.

Following their construction in 1799, the platinum meter and kilogram standards were put in protective containers and placed on deposit in the Institut National des Sciences et des Arts, in Paris. Iron copies of these two standards were supposed to be made and distributed to various regions of France, but they never were.

In spite of the 1795 law, the French public did not like the new metric system. The people felt more at ease with the old system. The old weights and measures (even though they were varied and complex) were efficient enough for their simple requirements.

In addition, the French people disliked the Greek and

Latin names of the new weights and measures. They had neither the time nor the desire to learn their meaning. Only scientists, engineers, and government workers showed any favor toward the metric system. The government people had little choice in the matter even if they did not like the metric measures since it was their duty to carry out instructions and set an example for others.

During the period immediately following the passage of the law in 1795, no real effort was made by the government to have the metric system accepted and used by the public. This lax attitude may have been due to the fact that the government was in a confused state and about to experience another radical change. Napoleon Bonaparte had arrived on the French scene and kept political affairs in a turmoil until he became entrenched in power. Under these circumstances it was hardly to be expected that a matter of such minor political importance as weights and measures should arouse any attention.

But as the years passed and Napoleon became the head of France, government officials found time to turn their interests to the everyday affairs of the people. This included the new system of measurements.

After some consideration of the almost total indifference of the public toward the metric system, the government under Napoleon decided there would be nothing wrong if the old and new systems of measures existed legally side by side. And so in 1812 a decree was issued that permitted the old system of measures to regain the same legal status as the metric system. The old measures were to be redefined in terms of metric standards, but to keep their old names.

Curiously enough, much of the original antagonism of the French people toward the metric system had disappeared by the time of the 1812 decree. This change had come about because the people had, to a surprising degree, blended the old with the new system of measures. What the people had done was to invent a kind of hybrid language of measures, adapting the old names of many of the different measurement units to the metric numerical values.

When the 1812 law went into effect it brought smiles of relief to the faces of merchants and others in the business world. They were the ones who, more than others, had to contend with the public's resistance toward the metric system. Now their job was easier, even though the twin systems of measures meant more complications in the selling of their products since the government now required that their scales be marked with both metric values and those of the old system.

Although the Bonaparte government was tolerant of the reluctance of the French people to accept and use the metric system — even legally allowing the old measures to continue — it was not so agreeable about the matter outside France. Wherever Napoleon's troops entered and conquered a country in Europe, decrees were issued to make the defeated people live according to certain French ways. This included the acceptance and use of the metric system.

Holland, in 1810, was one of the first to feel Napoleon's authority with respect to using the metric system. Apparently the Hollanders appreciated the advantages offered by the new system of measures and took to it readily. They have used it ever since. Their Belgian neighbors were introduced to metric measures shortly thereafter and here too it eventually became firmly established.

The metric system did not move across Europe on the point of bayonets alone. Information concerning the new language of measures made its way around by more peaceful methods. Travelers, exchange of letters, and newspaper accounts eventually spread the word about the simplicity and uniformity of the metric language of measures. Gradually, as its merits became better appreciated, metric measurement found a widening circle of acceptance.

Just as in France, scientists and people working in technical fields were the first to approve and accept the metric system. Indeed, it was mainly through the urgings of scientists that some of the cantons (states) of Switzerland adopted the metric system in 1801 as the legal standard of measures.

Another of the areas in Europe voluntarily to accept the metric system was the city-state of Milan, in 1803. (At that time, what we now know as Italy was a fragmented region of small kingdoms and city-states.) The people in Switzerland and Milan took to the metric measures a little more agreeably than Frenchmen because government authorities from the beginning had allowed the mixing of a few of the names of the old system with the new values. In time, however, the old names faded away as the metric system of weights and measures took over completely.

In the early nineteenth century, Germany was also, like Italy, partitioned into a number of small kingdoms. One of these, Baden, voluntarily adopted the metric system in 1810, becoming another member of the slowly growing family of those using metric weights and measures.

Whether by Napoleon's armies or more peaceful means, the use of the metric system spread steadily throughout Europe during the first half of the nineteenth century. There was growth of international trade during this period, and a greatly increased desire for such trade. But the lack of uniformity in weights and measures had long been recognized by government and business people as a hindrance to the free movement of goods. Now it looked as though the use of the metric system would remove this barrier.

Another event had a good deal to do with advancing the cause of the metric system throughout Europe. The government of France realized that the dual system of weights and measures that had existed since 1812 was not working out well. One or the other of the systems had to be chosen as the sole language of measures. The metric system won out.

On January 1, 1840, a French law went into effect that once again made the metric measures the sole legal standard of weights and measures in France. Frenchmen were now required by the new law to learn and use only metric measurements. To indicate that it meant business this time, the government included in the law a series of fines that would have to be paid by those caught using the old measures. Now there was no turning back. The country that gave the metric system to the world not only adopted and used the language of metric measures wholeheartedly, but also exercised strong efforts to spread its superior qualities elsewhere. As we shall see, this missionary work carried far beyond the shores of Europe — to America and other areas of the world as well.

4

The United States and the Language of Measurements

When the British colonists came to America they brought with them most of the traditions and ways of living that had been familiar to them in the mother country — including the British system of weights and measures. And the transplanted system of measurements was, of course, no clearer or simpler than it had been in England. Matters were not helped any by the fact that colonizing in America was a continuing process, spanning a period of many decades. Newcomers brought different units of weights and measures

American colonists used weights and measures brought from England. These settlers are using a knotted rope to find the correct length of the logs for use in building their house in the background.

at different times, as these were changed in England. The new measurement units were added to those already in use in the colonies, and the system became one of great variety. But it remained basically British.

For example, in the American colonies as in England, the foot was 12 inches; the fathom was 6 feet; the rod was 3½ yards; the furlong was 220 yards, and the mile 8 furlongs, or 5,280 feet. For measuring the volume of wheat, the colonists in America made use of the Winchester bushel, which had its origins in fifteenth-century England; for the gallon measure they used a wine gallon of 231 cubic inches, dating originally from about the thirteenth century, but made legal by Queen Anne of England in 1707.

After the American Revolution, when the British colonies had become the United States of America, the founders of the new nation realized that an efficient system of weights and measures, and coinage too, was needed for the government to conduct its affairs properly. Such a system was also needed for the day-to-day activities of the people.

The United States gallon is based on the British wine gallon standardized by Queen Anne in 1707.

The creators of the Constitution therefore included in this document Article I, Section 8: "Congress shall have power ... to coin money, regulate the value thereof, and of foreign coin, and fix the standard of weights and measures."

And George Washington, in his inaugural address, reminded the Congress of its responsibility for creating an efficient coinage and weights and measures system: ". . . uniformity in the currency, weights, and measures of the United States is an object of the greatest importance, and will, I am persuaded, be duly attended to."

Since money was used by everyone nearly every day, Congress gave the question of coinage immediate attention. They enlisted the help of Thomas Jefferson, asking him to study the subject and submit to Congress a plan for a national coinage system. The arrangement he created was based on the decimal system (dollar, dime, cent). He chose the factor of 10 for his coinage ratios because, in his words, ". . . the most easy ratio of multiplication and division is that by ten . . ."

The members of this country's first elected Congress approved Jefferson's plan, and speedily adopted it as the national coinage system in 1785. This put an end to the awkward and complicated use of British pence, halfpence, shillings, farthings, crowns, and pounds, and Jefferson's system is the one we have to this day.

While the first Congress acted promptly in establishing a coinage system, they performed with far less haste on the matter of a system of weights and measures. Here, too, Congress turned to Thomas Jefferson, requesting him to make a study of a system of measures and, if possible, to offer recommendations for the lawmakers to act upon. Jefferson, secretary of state at the time, dutifully accepted the assignment. In his usual intelligent, efficient way Jefferson produced two possible plans for the Congress to consider in 1790.

The first of these was the less drastic: it was simply a system to ". . . define and render uniform and stable . . ." in

Jefferson's words, the weights and measures of the English system which the people already commonly used.

A key element in Jefferson's scheme was to base a length standard on some occurrence in nature that could be uniformly and accurately reproduced, rather than on such variables as a kernel of barley or wheat, which had served as common standards for ages past.

Jefferson's proposal for a uniform length standard was a cylindrical iron rod that would swing back and forth as a pendulum. Its length would be such that a swing from one end of the arc it described to the other end and then back to the original point would take exactly 2 seconds. The device would also have to be located at a latitude of 45 degrees, at sea level, at a place where the temperature would be uniform over the course of a year.

Jefferson had learned of Talleyrand's idea for a basic unit of the metric system while traveling in France. Once such a length standard was established, Jefferson believed it would be a simple matter to derive from it consistently related units of area, volume, weight, and force, as well as other needed measurements.

But it was Jefferson's second plan that he favored and hoped Congress would accept. This involved discarding the old weights and measures altogether, and basing new ones on decimal ratios, similar to the coinage system he had created, because of the tremendous advantage gained by the ease of converting values by means of the factor of 10. This concept was not too far removed from the French metric system of weights and measures that was being developed at about the same time.

People really don't like big changes in what they are used to. Jefferson knew that there would be opposition to *any* new system of measures. However, he felt that by keeping as many old names as possible for the new units of weight and measurement, objections would be held to a minimum. Acceptance might also be helped by the fact that both the new measurement system and the country's coinage would

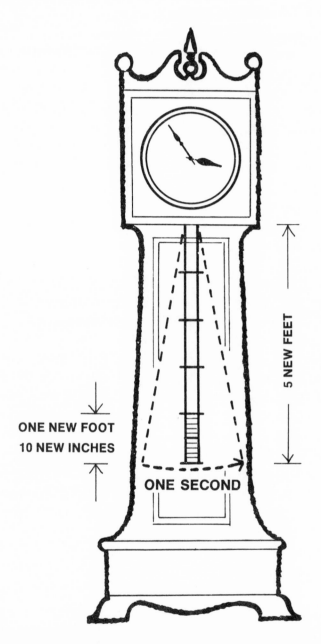

This drawing shows Thomas Jefferson's pendulum proposal for determining the length standard in his new system of weights and measures.

be based on decimal values. The decimal measurements plan, in Jefferson's mind, would simply be a logical extension of the decimal coinage concept.

Thus, using the factor of 10, Jefferson worked out linear measurements based on the length of the cylindrical iron rod ticking seconds (the rod would have been about 5 feet long, by today's measurements). The length of the rod was to be divided into five equal parts, each part to be called 1 foot. The major units of his linear measurements were as follows:

MULTIPLES	SUBMULTIPLES
10 feet = 1 decad	1/10 foot = 1 inch
10 decads = 1 rood	1/10 inch = 1 line
10 roods = 1 furlong	1/10 line = 1 point
10 furlongs = 1 mile	

Jefferson's decimal system would have had an ounce for its basic unit of weight. An ounce would have been equivalent to the weight of a cube of rainwater measuring 1/10 foot on each side. Ten ounces, not 16, would equal a pound.

As for capacity measures, Jefferson proposed a 1-cubic-foot bushel as the basic unit. This was to be the equivalent of a cubic foot of rainwater weighing 100 pounds, or 1,000 ounces.

Thomas Jefferson was firmly convinced that his new system of weights and measures would, to use his words, "... reduce every branch to the same decimal ratio already established for coin, and thus bring calculations of the principal affairs of life within the arithmetic of every man who can multiply and divide plain numbers." He was confident the Congress would act upon these proposals with the same speed as they had upon his coinage proposal.

President Washington, as a former surveyor, had an especially keen interest in the development of an efficient system of measures. In the next six years, he reminded the lawmakers twice to take some action on Jefferson's proposals. The members of Congress thought Jefferson's ideas were most interesting, but the proposals were turned over to a commit-tee for study, and there they ultimately died. Perhaps the feeling of the first elected Congress was that the people were getting along well enough with the measures in use and there was little need to complicate their daily affairs with a system so drastically different.

Many experts in the field of metrology feel today that it is too bad the first Congress did not have the foresight to adopt Jefferson's decimal scheme for weights and measures. If they had, the use of measures in the daily activities of the people would have been much simpler and easier. They would not have had to remember so many different units, or so many different values for calculation and conversion pur-poses. Over the period of two centuries since this nation's beginning, it would have meant a saving of countless mill-ions of dollars in the daily and commercial activities of the people, and in educational costs.

What might be described as the first bit of action on the part of the Congress to improve this country's system of measures took place in 1799. The action was not a very seri-ous effort, at that. It began with a problem concerning import duties that was causing a considerable loss of money to an anemic national treasury. It seems that at the nation's ports of entry customs inspectors had no standards of weights with which to impose a duty charge. Weights varied from port to port. Congress thought of a simple solution: it passed a law stating that there was to be a standard of weights at all the ports of entry.

But it was one thing to proclaim by law and quite another to have the law acted upon. Congress failed to provide the necessary machinery, such as a scientific group, to determine what the standards should be. It is possible that the Congress did nothing about this phase of the problem because there was little if any money in the national treasury with which to finance such an investigation.

Two events occurred in the early nineteenth century that were closely related to the problem of a lack of American measurement standards. Both involved Ferdinand Rudolph Hassler, a Swiss mathematician and an expert in geodesy. In 1807 he was engaged by the U.S. Government to head a group for surveying this country's coastline. However, his appointment was officially delayed until 1816, at which time he took over leadership of the newly organized U.S. Coast and Geodetic Survey.

Hassler remained in his job for only two years. He lost his position after the government decided that civilians were not to be allowed in coast survey work for reasons of military defense. Then in 1832 the rule was changed once more, again permitting civilians to participate in this specialized work. Because of his broad knowledge of the subject of geodesy, Hassler resumed his position as head of the survey workers.

When Hassler arrived in the United States in 1805, he had brought with him an iron bar copy of the original French meter standard. As director of the U.S. Coast and Geodetic Survey, he made this meter the standard of length for the work of the Geodetic Survey.

Geodetic survey workers dealt with precise measurements of the earth's surface, using the data gathered to determine the boundaries of the United States. They also wanted to record changes taking place in this nation's terrain, especially its coasts, which were constantly being modified by nature through storms and erosions. To perform their work properly, Coast and Geodetic surveyors needed an exact and uniform standard with which to obtain measurements. Hassler's iron bar meter standard was a great help, and was referred to as late as 1890 for all base measurements made by survey workers.

While in Europe once again in 1814, Hassler had made an 82-inch bronze bar with an inlaid silver scale. It was the work of an instrument maker, Troughton of London. The distance between the 27th and 63rd inches on the scale, 36 inches, was supposed to represent the English yard standard at 62 degrees Fahrenheit. Brought to the United States, this bar was also used for survey measurements. Later, from 1832 to 1856, the so-called Troughton bar was recognized unofficially as the standard of yard length throughout the country.

Toward the beginning of the nineteenth century, the nation's fourth president, James Madison, prodded Congress again to enact a law clarifying the system of weights and measures. While the general public seemed to be managing with the measurements then in use, a lack of standards was still causing a good deal of difficulty among the country's customs collectors.

As it had years earlier, Congress chose to ignore President Madison's urging. But during the administration of the next President, James Monroe, lawmakers decided it was time to give the matter some attention. In 1817 the Congress sent a request to the secretary of state, John Quincy Adams, to investigate the whole subject of weights and measures. In his report Adams was also to make suggestions for Congress to act upon.

Adams was a scholarly man and undertook the assignment with considerable satisfaction. He explored the subject in such depth that it took him four years to complete the task. Adams entitled his study "Report upon Weights and Measures" and sent it on to Congress in 1821. Four years later he became the nation's sixth President. In a way his measures report may have helped Adams attain that high office. It certainly added to his reputation as a man of considerable intellectual abilities.

The study Adams made not only presented an exhaustive background of the early history of weights and measures, but also included the first serious consideration of the use of the metric system for the United States. In his time the metric system had become established in France and was beginning to make its slow way across Europe. As to whether the United States should or should not adopt the metric system, Adams presented the pros and cons with equal emphasis. In later decades when the subject of metric measures for the United States provoked heated debate, the supporters of both sides of the question found substantial help in Adams's report.

John Quincy Adams was enormously impressed with the metric system. He liked especially its simplicity and uniformity for determining the values of its various units. Adams expressed his enthusiasm for metric measures in the following words: "... the establishment of such a system so obviously tends to that great result (benefiting mankind in his daily intercourse with his fellow men) the improvement of the physical, moral and intellectual condition of man upon earth; that there can be neither doubt or hesitancy in the opinion that the ultimate adoption and universal, though modified, application of that system is a consummation devoutly to be wished."

Adams found several features of the metric system that he considered outstanding advantages. Among these were the "invariable" standard of length that the system's creators had taken from nature, the single unit for weight and the single unit for volume, both of which were based on the length standard and equally invariable, the decimal basis of the system's various unit values, and, finally but by no means least important, the metric system's uniform and precise terminology.

But Adams also had some reservations about the metric system. The advantage of using single units for *all* measures of weight and capacity was really no advantage, in his opinion. Such measures, he felt, could not take into account the natural differences in the objects to be weighed and measured, as the old multiple units had. Thus the gallon of corn had been established as different from the gallon of wine because the measures by which solid and liquid substances were sold could not be conveniently united to fill the everyday needs of the people.

Even though the metric system's decimal base was considered by Adams as "one of its highest theoretic excellencies," he did not think it was working out among the

French people. It would have been more practical for general trade purposes, he felt, if a base-12 system were used. This could be evenly divided by 2, 3, 4, and 6, while the number 10 is only divisible by 2 and 5.

Finally, Adams believed that the new names chosen for the various metric units were too great a handicap. After all, he pointed out, these had not yet been accepted by the French people. A similar difficulty could be expected from the American public.

Along with a detailed account of the metric system and his own judgment of it, Adams included in his report four possible courses of action the members of Congress might take with respect to improving the system of measurements in the United States.

Congress, he suggested, could "adopt in all its essential parts the new French system of weights and measures."

Or Congress could "restore and perfect the old English system of weights, measures, moneys and silver coins."

Or it was possible to "devise and establish a (combined) system. . . by adoption of parts of each system to the principles of the other."

Or, finally, Adams advised Congress that it could "adhere, without any innovation whatever, to our existing weights and measures, merely fixing standards."

If the federal lawmakers were interested in Adams's personal recommendation on what action should be taken he volunteered that too. Adams would first have had the familiar English units standardized and approved without change. Then, later, he would have had the President of the United States enter into negotiations with the heads of government of France, Great Britain, and Spain for the purpose of establishing a uniform international measurement system. In view of the already existing metric system in France, its steady acceptance by other countries, and Adams's own enthusiasm for its eventual adoption, it is probably what the statesman had in mind for international usage.

After Adams submitted his study to Congress in 1821, he

waited with some interest to see what the lawmakers would do about it. True to form, Congress did nothing. The Adams report was referred to a committee for consideration and there it became lost in the shuffle of bills on other matters.

In 1832, there was again a slight flurry of congressional action on the matter of weights and measures. This was triggered by that seemingly perennial problem of a lack of standards at the various customhouses throughout the country. Since the Congress had done nothing about this in previous years, the customs problem just kept rolling along in its mixed-up state until complaints again became so loud and frequent that the lawmakers were forced into action.

The Congress sent the problem over to the secretary of the treasury this time to make a study and recommendations, since by this time the Treasury had been given control over affairs dealing with duties on imports. In its efforts to deal with the task given it by Congress, the Treasury Department borrowed Ferdinand Hassler from the Coast and Geodetic Survey. Hassler was directed not only to investigate the problem but also to prepare a set of standards for possible use.

Hassler handled his assignment quickly and efficiently. First he obtained an overall picture of the confused system of measures used at the customhouses scattered throughout the nation. The standards of length and capacity were every bit as varied as Congress had been informed they were. Then the engineer proceeded to draw up a set of standards which he believed were sufficiently uniform for use at the customhouses along the Atlantic Coast, and the Gulf Coast, and in the Great Lakes region. To arrive at these standards, Hassler borrowed heavily from the English measurement system.

He defined the various units of length with the help of the Troughton bar. He defined the different units of weight using the brass troy pound standard which the United States Mint had also imported from England.

Although Hassler worked with standards that had originated in England, some of them were in fact no longer used there. For example, the gallon standard adopted by Hassler was the Queen Anne's wine gallon, with a volume of 231 cubic inches. But England had given that up in 1824 for the so-called imperial gallon, which was slightly larger.

It was the same with the standard for the bushel. Hassler had chosen the old Winchester standard, equal to 2,150.42 cubic inches, still in common use in the United States but no longer in England. Our bushel was slightly lower in capacity than the newer imperial British unit.

In due course the standards for length, weight (or mass), and volume worked out by Hassler were constructed and sent to the various customhouses throughout the country. They were also submitted by the federal government to all the state governments for possible adoption. Such adoption was strictly a voluntary matter since state governments in the early nineteenth century were even more sensitive about their legislative prerogatives than they are today. In the absence of any national system of weights and measures, such as existed for coinage, many of the states had established their own standards for measurements.

As matters turned out, no real difficulties developed. Over a period of years the measurement units developed by Hassler were adopted by the states. Thus, for the first time, the United States acquired a uniform system of weights and measures.

Even though Congress had busied itself with the subject of weights and measures in 1832, there was little general interest in the matter. At that time and for the next several decades preceding the Civil War, the country was involved with far more serious political problems, slavery for one. It was a time that also witnessed a great expansion throughout the land in population, industry, and agriculture. In short, the United States was busily engaged with all the activities of a fast-growing giant.

When the subject of the nation's need for a more precise

and uniform language of weights and measures was occasionally brought up, it was usually in academic or scientific circles. There was little doubt how most of the individuals in both these groups felt on the matter. They were highly in favor of the metric system and would have liked to see its adoption by the United States. However, since they were small in number and had limited influence in public affairs, their opinions on the metric system caused hardly a ripple of attention.

When the Civil War came, though, there was a surprising change. For the first time since John Quincy Adams had referred to it in his report, the metric system became a lively and prominent topic of discussion.

This new development began in 1863, when President Abraham Lincoln established the National Academy of Sciences. The purpose of organizing the scientists into this special group was to advise the federal government on matters of technical interest, both military and nonmilitary. Among the more peaceful assignments given the scientists of the Academy was the investigation of ways to improve the nation's system of weights and measures. The committee of Academy members appointed to undertake this task was headed by Joseph Henry, an outstanding physicist of that era and the first president of the Smithsonian Institution.

The committee completed its study in two years and issued a report with recommendations. The most important of these was that the country should abandon its old English standards of measures for the far more efficient metric system. The study and its recommendations were then turned over to a newly formed committee of the House of Representatives, the Committee on Coinage, Weights, and Measures. Chairman of the group was Congressman John A. Kasson of Iowa.

Congressman Kasson and his colleagues on the committee were obviously believers in action. After warmly approving the report of the Academy scientists, the committee prepared and sent three bills relating to the metric system to the floor of the House of Representatives for that body to consider and vote upon. This was in 1866.

The most important of the three bills permitted the legal use of the metric system in this country along with the customary measures. In addition, this particular bill also allowed English system equivalents to be used with the metric weights and measures. The second of the committee bills directed the postmaster general to provide metric postal scales to all post offices exchanging mail with foreign countries. Finally, the third bill directed the secretary of the treasury to furnish each state with a set of metric standards.

In the committee's favorable report to Congress for passage of these bills, Chairman Kasson was careful to point out that there was no compulsion attached to these laws. They were to be adopted by the people of the country on a purely voluntary basis. Perhaps because of this feature, Congress went along with the committee's recommendations and passed all three bills.

This is considered the first official action that established a relationship between this country and the metric system. Even though the passage of these three measures fell far short of what advocates of the metric language favored in the way of strong, positive action, they were encouraged. At least it was a step in the right direction. And perhaps, through education and the use of metric units along with the English equivalents, other steps would be taken that would lead eventually to full acceptance of the metric system.

By the early 1870s the subject of metric measures had become a popular topic of debate in the United States. Not surprisingly, much of this was centered among educators, some of whom were by no means in favor of this country going metric. They believed the Anglo-Saxon system of measures to be a superior system, even though they were ready to admit it could stand improvement. A changeover to metric for the United States would only result in enormous (if temporary) financial loss to industry and commerce, and create untold confusion among the American people. The debate between the two opposing groups made people in this country much more aware of the metric system than they had been before.

One of the outstanding spokesmen against adopting the metric system was Professor Charles Davies, of Columbia College. Professor Davies had been chairman of a committee charged with the task of exploring what might be done to increase public awareness of the metric system. At the conclusion of their work, the committee members recommended that nothing should be done. They felt that if the United States were to abandon its customary system of measures for the metric, the change would bring only chaos to the nation's commercial life and the affairs of the people in general.

Dr. Frederick A. P. Barnard, president of Columbia College, was a strong metric booster. He read the Davies committee report with mounting indignation. Then he sat down and wrote a strong counterattack. He enumerated the ways by which he thought the public should be informed about the superior features of metric measures. If the matter were to be left to the Columbia College president, he would have had the metric system taught in all the schools in the country. Metric measures would also be used for the formation of tariff laws and in the establishment of customs duties. Finally, Dr. Barnard would have had various departments of the federal government employ metric measures on a compulsory basis, in such areas as public surveys, army and naval activities, and the country's post offices.

Feeling so strongly in favor of the metric system, Dr. Barnard went beyond merely publicizing his ideas on the subject; he also organized the American Metrological Society in 1873, with himself as president. The aim of the society was to promote the cause of metric measures in every possible way. Many prominent people in government — Congressman John A. Kasson for one — in education, and in science became active members of the society. Under Dr. Barnard's vigorous leadership the society launched an enthusiastic publicity campaign, through the use of lectures and articles in the newspapers and magazines, to arouse the American public's interest in and support for the metric system.

As the society became increasingly involved with its educational activities, many members thought their efforts ought to be widened. During the late nineteenth century intercourse between nations, both in the new world and the old, was increasing at a rapid rate. As a result of this development, these members of the society felt that a vigorous educational effort, similar to that for a metric system, should also be made for the establishment of international uniform coinage and standardized time zones.

This feeling was not shared by Dr. Ferdinand Barnard. He believed that the society should confine its work to the adoption of the metric system, and that to divide the society's interest with other matters would simply weaken the effort toward the main objective. He felt so strongly about this that in 1876 he resigned from the society to form a new group, the American Metric Bureau, and became its president.

Dr. Barnard now devoted almost all his spare time to promoting interest in metric measures among the American people. One of his assistants was a young librarian, Melvil Dewey. In a few years Dewey was destined to achieve considerable international fame in his own right, by creating a decimal system for classifying library books. Today, the Dewey decimal system is in almost universal use in libraries throughout the world.

One of the major programs that the American Metric Bureau embarked upon was the purchase of scales, rules, and capacity measures based on metric values. These were sold to schools at a nominal price, in an effort to introduce the advantages of metric measures to the uninformed. The program continued as long as the Bureau had funds with which to buy, then sell, metric instruments and materials to educational institutions. Funds were acquired through membership fees, lectures and writings of members, and public contributions from people who were in sympathy with the work of the Bureau. But when finances dry up, the activities of many causes slow down and in time stop completely. This was the end of the Bureau, hastened by Dr. Barnard's death in 1889.

The promotional work of both the American Metric Bureau and its parent, the American Metrological Society, succeeded to a considerable degree in stimulating general

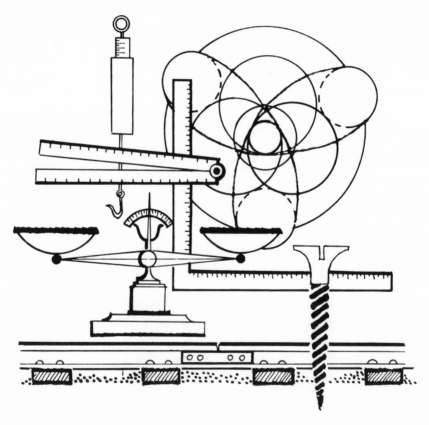

Weights and measures play a part in just about all of man's activities.

public interest in the metric system. But there was also some extremely vocal opposition to change in the country's customary measurement system.

One group that came into existence to counter the work of the metric advocates was the International Institute for Preserving and Perfecting Weights and Measures. It was formed in 1879 by Charles Latimer, an engineer from Cleveland, Ohio. With headquarters in Boston (to be near their adversaries), Latimer and his followers launched a series of programs that strongly denounced the arguments of the prometric people. They based their case mainly on the opinions of those who had opposed the metric system earlier. These included the firm belief that there was nothing basically wrong with the system of weights and measures then in use; also, any changeover to metric would be economically disastrous and produce untold confusion among the general public.

The economic loss referred to would include the cost of replacing or recalibrating all existing rulers, yardsticks, and scales; and, more significant, possible changes in important capital goods, for example, the gauge of railroad tracks, as well as in the thread of screws, size of machine parts, and so on. However, the British experience has shown that these fears were exaggerated, as we will see later.

As the nineteenth century ended and the twentieth century began, advocates of the metric system had experienced both advances and reverses, but they still had not lost hope of one day achieving their objective.

5

The Metric System:
Refinement and Expansion

During the nineteenth century, the use of the metric system spread among the nations of Europe and South America. But science and technology were developing extremely rapidly in the western world, and the metric language did not provide all the new standards of measurements which scientists and technologists now required. As a result, they were among the first to point out the necessity for refining and expanding the system of metric measures.

Primarily on the initiative of the French scientists, Emperor Napoleon III sent invitations to the nations of Europe and the Americas to attend a conference at Paris for the purpose of improving the metric system. Twenty-four nations accepted, including the United States and Great Britain who were nonusers of the system. Delegates gathered in August 1870. Their first order of business was to form themselves into an international commission. The main task of the commission was to discuss and arrange for the construction of a new prototype meter and kilogram. Also, it was to make arrangements for giving each of the nations represented at the conference a duplicate set of the new standards.

The outbreak of war between France and Germany

brought a sudden end to the work of the commission. It wasn't until September 1872 that the delegates resumed their activities. This time there were thirty nations represented, with fifty-one commission members, including some of the world's leading scientists. Among the distinguished members of the American delegation was Joseph Henry, head of the National Academy of Sciences and former chairman of its committee on weights, measures, and coinage.

The work of the commission was drawn out by successive meetings over a period of several years. By 1875 it had resolved the problems relating to the design and construction of the new standards. The delegates had also recommended establishment of an international bureau of weights and measures. A permanent committee was appointed to carry out the commission's recommendations, especially the one relating to the construction of the new meter and kilogram standards.

At the request of the members of the permanent committee the French government called a conference of high government officials of various countries interested, who would consider ways of verifying the new standards recommended by the commission, as well as methods of storing and preserving them. Nineteen nations, including the United States, sent diplomats to this conference, which took place in March 1875. Two months later they completed their work with the Treaty of the Meter. Seventeen of the nineteen countries signed it. The most important of the treaty's points called for the establishment and maintenance of a permanent International Bureau of Weights and Measures to be located near Paris. The bureau was to be controlled by an international committee of fourteen members from different countries. The United States ratified this treaty on September 27, 1878, in spite of some strong opposition from antimetric groups.

The bureau was to take charge of the construction and

verification of the new meter and kilogram standards. Also, when these international prototypes were completed, the bureau was to see to their proper storage and preservation. The bureau was given additional responsibilities of making periodic comparisons of several national metric standards with the international prototypes, and of comparing metric standards with different nonmetric standards of other countries.

The activities of the International Bureau were to be supervised by a General Conference on Weights and Measures, which would meet every six years to decide questions of importance dealing with the metric system. The work of the bureau was also to be the responsibility of a permanent International Committee of Weights and Measures, meeting every two years. This arrangement of international groups for keeping the metric system up-to-date continues to the present day.

To house the new bureau, the French government provided land and a building, a former royal estate near Sèvres. This was not too far from Paris. The building was

At one time an X-shaped metal bar made of platinum and iridium and of a precise length served as the standard for the meter. A number of copies were made and distributed to various countries. The United States obtained bars numbered 21 and 27.

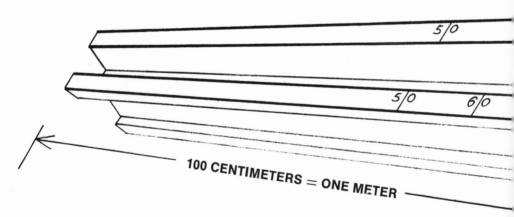

renovated for the work of the staff, and with Gilberto Govi, an Italian physicist, as its first director the bureau began its duties in the new quarters in 1878.

The measures and weights experts of the bureau had already started, in 1877, to carry out their assignment to construct new physical meter and kilogram standards. This task was not an easy one and the new standards were not completed until 1889. The principal difficulties were in obtaining the necessary quantities of extremely high-purity platinum-iridium alloy, the material the members of the commission had requested for forming the standards. They felt this new alloy would make for more stable physical standards, the meter bar in particular. Even though the original of this had changed its shape only very slightly, it was enough to interfere with its use as an exact and uniform measure.

Another problem concerned the way in which the meter standard and its duplicates were made. Again on instructions from commission members, each standard bar was to be constructed from a single ingot and in one casting. Its design

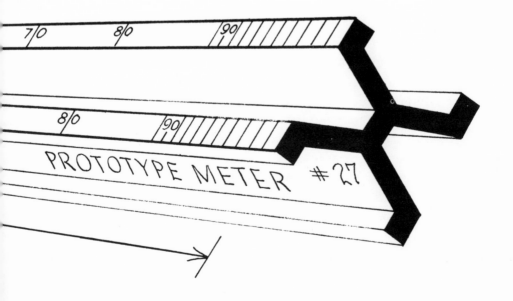

was to be a unique X-shape in cross section. The standard had then to be carefully heat-treated for hardening. Many failures were experienced before final, satisfactory units were produced. There were thirty-one meter standard bars made, and forty kilogram standards. They were stamped with numbers for identification.

After the international prototypes were selected and placed in the vaults of the International Bureau of Weights and Measures near Paris, the other nations drew lots for their duplicate sets. The United States drew meter bars numbered 21 and 27, and kilogram standards numbered 4 and 20. They were brought to this country in 1890.

Following the signing of the Treaty of the Meter (1878), which the United States had helped to bring into existence, the U.S. secretary of the treasury issued an administrative order in 1893 stating that from that time onward the new metric standards would serve as this country's "fundamental standards" of length and mass (weight). The yard, the pound, and all the other customary units of weights and measures were to be defined as fractions of the standard metric units. With this action, the United States became in one sense a metric nation. But, even though this was a major step toward United States adoption of metric measurements, it did not mean that the normally used units for the foot, the pound, or other measurements were to be abandoned. It simply meant that for accurate, comparative purposes, the metric standards were to be used over any others.

Events that took place after the 1870-75 meeting of the International Commission proved definitely that the metric system was not static. Its language was flexible enough to adjust to changes and additions. The metric system could readily accommodate new measurement standards as the advancement of science and the expansion of industry and commerce showed the need for them.

From the metric system's two original basic units all measurements for length, area, volume, capacity, and mass (weight) were derived. But as time passed, the number of basic units has increased.

The third basic unit of the metric system was added to it by the General Conference meeting in 1891. It was a unit of time and was designated as the *second*.

It was not until the General Conference get-together of 1950 that the fourth basic metric unit, the *ampere*, was chosen as the standard measure of electric current. This was due largely to the efforts of Professor Giovanni Giorgi, an Italian physicist. In 1935 he had recommended that a fourth unit be added to the metric system to serve as a link between the fields of mechanics and electromagnetics. For this fourth unit he had suggested the ampere, coulomb, ohm, or volt. The ampere was selected as the new standard.

Meeting again in 1954, the General Conference on Weights and Measures agreed to add two more base units to the modern metric system. These were the *Kelvin*, a unit of temperature, and the *candela*, a unit of luminous intensity.

Several important decisions were made at the eleventh meeting of the General Conference of 1960. Delegates from thirty-six nations attended, including those from the United States. At this gathering the members voted to give the metric system an official name, Le Système International d'Unités, or the International System of Units. The abbreviation SI was also made official because the full title was too long for everyday use.

Also at this 1960 meeting of the General Conference, it was agreed to add two supplementary units to the basic units already selected. The newcomers were the *radian* (rad), a unit of measure of a plane angle, and the *steradian* (sr), a unit of measure of a solid angle.

When the General Conference met in 1964, the delegates made only a few minor adjustments to the system. Three years later the weights and measures experts had another meeting (outside of their six-year schedule), during which they redefined the unit of time (the second), renamed the unit of temperature by changing the capital *K* of Kelvin to lowercase, *kelvin* (K), and revised the definition of the candela.

In October of 1971, the seventh and last base unit was added to the modern metric system. This unit is the *mole* and represents the amount of a particular substance. Thus, the present metric system now has the name SI, seven basic units, two supplementary units, and a large family of derived units. The latter are defined in terms of the base units and are used only for special purposes.

QUANTITY	UNIT	SYMBOL
length	meter	m
mass (weight)	kilogram	kg
time	second	s
electric current	ampere	A
temperature	kelvin	K
luminous intensity	candela	cd
amount of substance	mole	mol

supplementary units:

plane angle	radian	rad
solid angle	steradian	sr

These are the foundation blocks on which the SI is built to provide a logical and interconnected structure for all measurements in science, industry, and commerce.

When the metric system was first developed, the original meter standard had been based on one ten-millionth of the length of a quadrant of the earth's meridian. More recently, after scientists were able to measure the earth's circumference with greater precision, the calculations of their eighteenth-century colleagues on which the meter standard was formulated were found to be inaccurate. The discrepancy was slight, on the order of 1 part in 3,000. Nevertheless, it was sufficient to send modern experts on

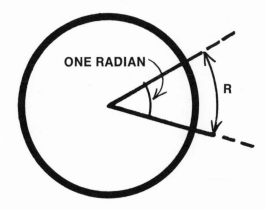

The radian, one of two supplementary units in the metric system, is defined as the plane angle with its vertex at the center of a circle that is subtended by an arc equal in length to the radius.

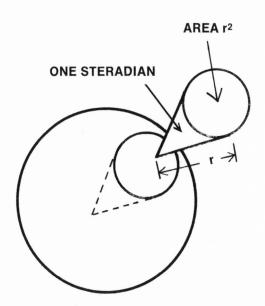

The steradian, second of the two supplementary units of the metric system, is defined as the solid angle with its vertex at the center of a sphere that is subtended by an area of the spherical surface equal to that of a square with sides equal in length to the radius.

weights and measures in search of a new, unchanging, and indestructible meter standard.

It was at the busy 1960 meeting of the General Conference that a new meter standard was discussed and adopted. The scientists in attendance agreed that the meter should now be the equivalent of 1,650,763.73 wavelengths in a vacuum of the orange-red light given off by a krypton 86 (Kr-86) atom. In the precise terms of the scientists, the definition is as follows: The meter is the length equal to 1,650,763.73 wavelengths in a vacuum of the radiation corresponding to the transition between levels $2p_{10}$ and $5d_5$ of the krypton 86 atom. Krypton 86 is an isotope of the inert gas krypton, which is found in small quantities in the earth's atmosphere.

The kilogram (kg), the standard of mass, or weight, has required no change since it was first made a part of the metric system. It is represented by the cylinder of platinum-iridium alloy stored in a vault at the International Bureau of Weights and Measures near Paris. An exact duplicate of this cylinder is in the vaults of the National Bureau of Standards in Washington, D.C. The kilogram was last reaffirmed as a base unit in 1901 at the third General Conference.

The standard for the basic unit of the second (s), like that

The standard for the meter, the unit of length in the metric system, is now determined with the help of an atomic device.

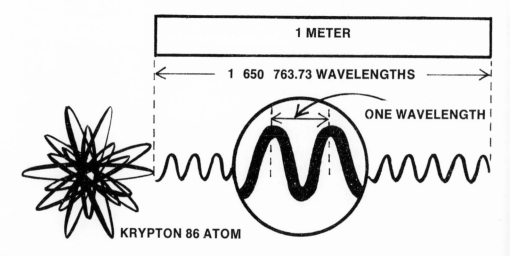

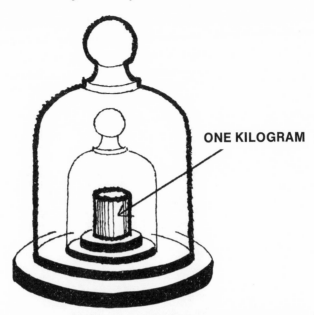

ONE KILOGRAM

The standard for the unit of mass, the kilogram, is a cylinder of platinum-iridium alloy kept by the International Bureau of Weights and Measures at Paris. A duplicate is at the National Bureau of Standards and serves as the mass standard for the United States. This is the only base unit of the metric system still defined by an artifact.

for the meter, has its origin in the atom. In earlier years the second was based on a unit of ephemeris time, which is related to the speed of the earth's rotation. But when scientists discovered that our planet's rotation varies, its use for a measurement standard was considered no longer applicable. A more precise way was found, with the help of the atomic clock, for deriving this base unit, and it was adopted by the General Conference in 1967.

According to the new definition, the second is equivalent to the duration of 9,192,631,770 cycles of the radiation related to a specific transition of the cesium-133 atom. To reproduce this in a laboratory, a source of cesium atoms is located at one end of an atomic beam spectrometer. The cesium source is bombarded by a powerful stream of atomic particles. This knocks the cesium atoms loose. These travel at a certain frequency. Magnets in the spectrometer cause the

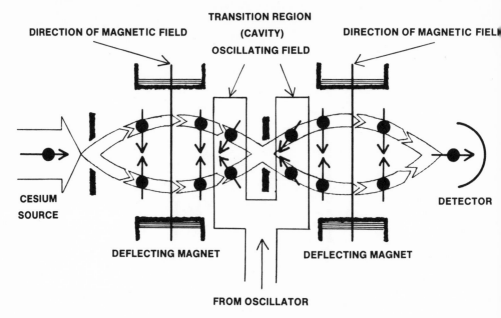

TRANSITION REGION
(CAVITY)
OSCILLATING FIELD

DIRECTION OF MAGNETIC FIELD

DIRECTION OF MAGNETIC FIELD

CESIUM
SOURCE

DETECTOR

DEFLECTING MAGNET

DEFLECTING MAGNET

FROM OSCILLATOR

This schematic drawing represents the second as the base unit of time in the metric system.

cesium atoms to move in a wave form. An oscillator guides the swift moving atoms through a detector at the end of the spectrometer. The detector records the peak of each cycle as it passes. With the recording of 9,192,631,770 of these cycles, a second has passed.

The ampere, joining the electromagnetic field with that

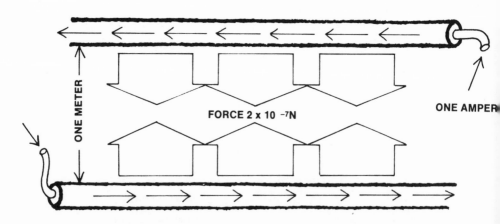

ONE METER

FORCE 2 x 10 $^{-7}$N

ONE AMPERE

The ampere is the base unit of electric current in the metric system.

of mechanics, is defined as the constant current which, if maintained in two straight parallel wires of infinite length and placed 1 meter apart in a vacuum, will produce between these wires a force (due to their magnetic fields) equal to 2×10^{-7} newtons for each meter of length. (A newton is one of the derived units of the metric system, about which more will be said shortly.)

The base unit for thermodynamic temperature is the kelvin (K), first included in the metric system in 1954, then revised by the thirteenth General Conference in 1967. The kelvin is now defined as the fraction 1/273.16 of the thermodynamic temperature of the triple point of water.

The "triple point of water" refers to the unique temperature at which water can exist in three states: liquid, vapor, and solid (ice). A laboratory device called a triple point cell is used to reproduce the triple state of water. It consists of a glass cylinder emptied of air and filled with pure water. This is placed within a larger cylindrical container in which there is a refrigerating element. The refrigerant cools the cell until a coating of ice forms around the cylinder. The temperature at the interface where the three states of water exist — liquid, vapor, and ice — is about 32.02 degrees on our familiar Fahrenheit scale. Thermometers to be calibrated are placed inside the triple point cell.

However, the Fahrenheit scale is not a part of the metric system. The metric system uses both the *Kelvin scale*, devised in the nineteenth century by the English physicist William Thompson (Lord Kelvin), and the *Celsius* or centigrade *scale*, named for Anders Celsius, the Swedish astronomer who first developed the centigrade thermometer in 1742.

The triple point of water is registered on the Celsius scale at 0.01 degree and on the Kelvin scale at 273.17 kelvins. The accompanying diagram shows the relationship of several major readings on all three scales, the Fahrenheit, Celsius, and Kelvin.

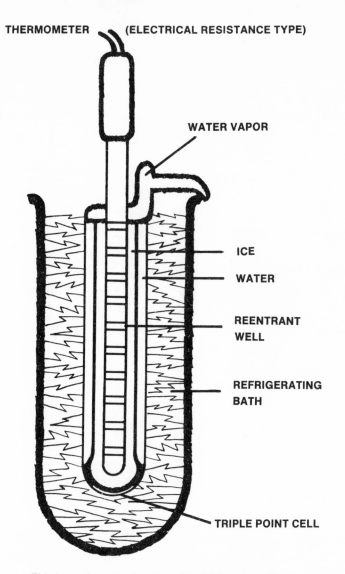

THERMOMETER (ELECTRICAL RESISTANCE TYPE)

WATER VAPOR

ICE

WATER

REENTRANT WELL

REFRIGERATING BATH

TRIPLE POINT CELL

This is a schematic drawing of the triple point cell.

The candela (cd), added to the modern metric system in 1967, measures luminous intensity. The candela has been defined as the luminous intensity, in the perpendicular direction, of 1/600,000 square meter of a cone of light radiated by a black body whose temperature has been made to equal 2,045 kelvins, the freezing point of platinum.

In SI language, the mole is the amount of a substance in a system that contains as many elementary entities as there are atoms in 0.012 kilogram of carbon 12. Most of us need not be too concerned with this base unit which was established and added to the metric system mainly for the work of physicists and chemists, especially in the study of solutions, as of salt in water.

We can see from the foregoing that the base units have

These are three principal temperature scales in current use. The drawing shows the relationship of their major readings.

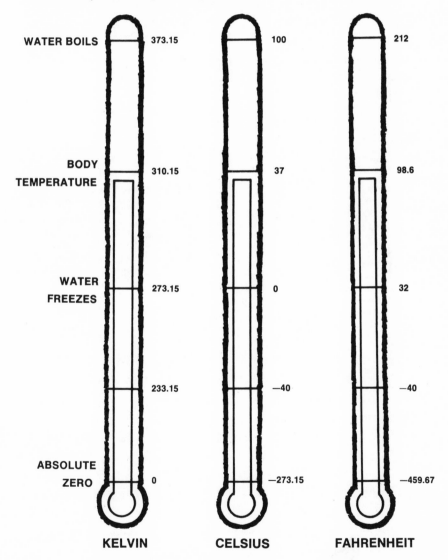

	KELVIN	CELSIUS	FAHRENHEIT
WATER BOILS	373.15	100	212
BODY TEMPERATURE	310.15	37	98.6
WATER FREEZES	273.15	0	32
	233.15	−40	−40
ABSOLUTE ZERO	0	−273.15	−459.67

LIGHT EMITTED HERE

CAVITY

FREEZING
PLATINUM

INSULATING
MATERIAL

This schematic drawing depicts the candela, the metric standard unit for luminous intensity.

The mole is the base unit in the metric system for the amount of a particular substance.

CARBON 12

been accurately defined by scientists, and, with the exception of the kilogram standard, which is considered an artifact, the physical measurements they represent can now easily be reproduced in any well-equipped physics laboratory any-place in the world. Thus, the modernized metric system has a degree of international uniformity impossible to achieve at an earlier time.

As mentioned earlier, in addition to the seven base units and two supplementary units of the current international metric system, there is a very large number of derived units.

Defined in terms of the basic units, derived units have also been given symbols for identification and, in some instances, special names.

Some of the more common derived units relate to area measurements. For small areas, square centimeters (cm²) are used. Larger areas are measured by the square meter (m²). The hectare (from the original metric base unit, the are) is employed to measure very large areas, as for land surveys. The hectare is 10,000 square meters, or about 2.5 acres in our measurements.

The physical quantity of volume has for its derived unit the cubic meter (m³). The cubic decimeter (dm³), referred to as the liter, is also a commonly used unit. Where smaller

This drawing shows a comparison between the metric liter and our liquid quart.

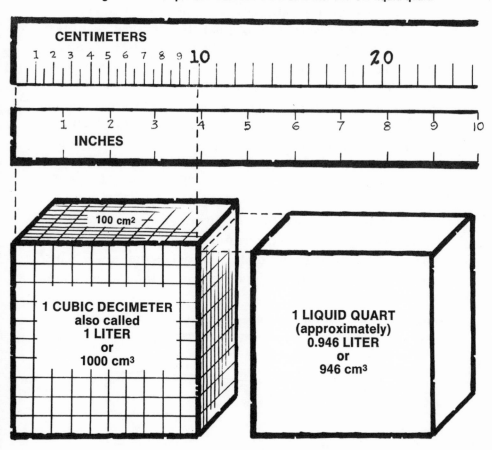

volume measurements are involved, as in dispensing drugs, or in scientific work, the cubic centimeter (cm³), also known as the milliliter, is preferred.

One of the derived units with a special name and definition is the *newton* (N), used for measurements of force in physics. The newton is defined as that force which, when applied to a body having a mass (weight) of 1 kilogram, gives it an acceleration of 1 meter per second per second (kg·m/s²). The newton is named, of course, for Isaac Newton, the famous British physicist and discoverer of one of nature's most elemental forces, gravity.

Another derived unit, the *hertz* (Hz), represents the physical quantity of frequency in the field of electromagnetism. By definition 1 hertz (Hz) simply equals 1 cycle per second. The term is named after Heinrich Rudolph Hertz, an outstanding German physicist of the nineteenth century.

The *joule* (J) is used to designate the physical quantity of energy. Energy comes in a variety of forms — heat, electrical, mechanical, chemical, and nuclear. To eliminate the need for individual names for the different kinds of energy, a single term, joule, was chosen to represent them all. The joule is defined as the work done when the point of application of a force of 1 newton is displaced a distance of 1 meter in the direction of the force. The joule may also be more simply expressed as 1 newton meter. The joule is named after a renowned English physicist James Prescott Joule.

The physical quantity of power of any kind is represented by the derived SI unit, the watt (W). The watt is precisely defined in the metric system as the power which gives rise to the production of energy at the rate of 1 joule

The *newton* (N) is defined as that force which, when applied to a body having a mass of 1 kilogram, gives it an acceleration of 1 meter per second per second.

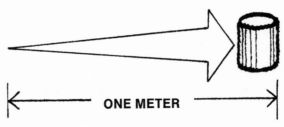

ONE METER

per second. This derived unit is named after James Watt of England, one of the early giants in the science of physics.

The SI derived unit for voltage is the *volt* (V), named for the Italian physicist Alessandro Volta. The volt is defined as the difference of electrical potential between two points of a conductor carrying constant current of 1 ampere, when the power used between these points is equal to 1 watt.

Another derived electrical unit is called the *ohm* (Ω). This is the unit of electrical resistance. Technically defined, the ohm is the electrical resistance between two points of a conductor when a constant difference of potential of 1 volt, applied between these two points, produces in this conductor a current of 1 ampere.

A number of other kinds of units exist that are not really a part of the modern metric system, although they are related to its units. These associated units are used in specialized branches of physics. For example, the *bar* is a unit of pressure and is commonly employed by meteorologists. Another unit is the *gal* (for Galileo), equal to an acceleration of 0.01 meter per second per second. Specialists in the field of geodetics make frequent use of this unit.

The modern international metric system (SI), as it has been developed, is now well arranged and very clear. Its seven base units, the bedrock of the system, are the source of all its other units of measurements. There exists a definite relationship between all the metric measurements.

In addition, one and only one unit is used to designate each of the physical quantities the system measures. The meter, for example, stands for length; the kilogram for mass (weight); and so forth.

One of the most important advantages of the metric language is the fact that it is based on the decimal system. The multiples and submultiples of any of its units are always related by powers of 10. There are 10 milliliters, for instance, in 1 centiliter, 100 centimeters in 1 meter, and 1,000 grams in 1 kilogram.

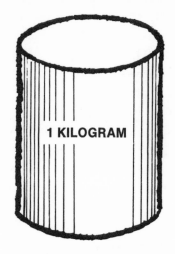

1 pound $=$ 0.453 592 37 kg

The kilogram and our pound measure are shown compared in this drawing.

This arrangement greatly simplifies the task of changing larger measurements into smaller measurements and vice versa. In many cases this involves no more than moving the decimal point to the right for obtaining smaller quantities, or to the left for larger quantities.

As an example, suppose we wish to find the number of meters in 2.873 kilometers. We multiply 2.873 by 1,000 by simply moving the decimal point three places to the right. The answer is 2,873 meters. By contrast, if we needed to know the number of inches in 2.873 miles we would first

The comparison between the metric meter and the yard measure is illustrated here.

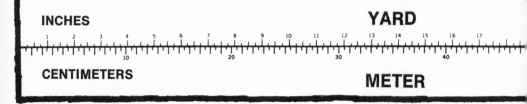

have to convert 2.873 miles into feet by multiplying by 5,280 — the number of feet to a mile. Then the resulting figure would have to be multiplied again, this time by 12, to get our desired answer in inches.

The decimal arrangement of the international metric system is further simplified by the use of consistent prefixes for all its multiples and submultiples. The familiar kilo-, for example, always stands for 1,000. When this is attached as a prefix to any unit of measure, we know immediately that the unit must be interpreted in terms of a thousand. One kilovolt equals 1,000 volts; 1 kilowatt equals 1,000 watts. Micro- always denotes one-millionth. One meter equals 1 million micrometers, 1 gram equals 1 million micrograms, and so on. (See Appendix 1 for a complete list of prefixes used with all SI units.)

The International System of Units (SI), which we commonly refer to as the metric system, is the only language of measurements that was ever created for universal use. Its wide acceptance since it was conceived almost two hundred years ago has put into the discard dozens of measurement systems that have complicated man's activities since time immemorial. With its logical arrangement, its simplicity, its uniformity, and, above all, its flexibility, it is in a real sense a living creation. The metric system seems assured, therefore, of remaining not only a universal language of measurements but also one that will continue to fulfill whatever demands are made upon it in the decades ahead.

6

The United States –
Last to Go Metric

Today more than 90 percent of the people of the world use
the metric system as their official language of measurements.
Over 75 percent of the world's industry, agricultural
production, and commerce is carried on with the use of the
metric system, and the trend is increasing annually. One of
the last of the major nations to join the world family of metric
users was Great Britain, in May 1965.

What caused England to abandon its complex system of
weights and measures rooted in centuries of cultural
development? There were a number of reasons, but the
principal one was probably economic necessity. By 1965
most of the nations of the world were alreaady using or were
about to use the metric system. English products manufactured to that country's imperial measurements were
finding an ever smaller market in international competition
with those made to metric standards. Countries using metric
measurements obviously found products made with metric
measurements a good deal more convenient, especially
when it came to repairs and the replacement of parts.

English government leaders had become more and more
aware of the measurements problem in the decades
following World War II. They decided that they had more to

One day when the United States adopts the metric system, housewives will find, as their British counterparts have, that there is no particular difficulty in buying food according to metric weight.

gain than to lose with a changeover from the long-used, familiar imperial measurements to those of the simpler metric system. The English planned to accomplish the conversion gradually over a period of ten years, to minimize as much as possible disruption in the daily affairs of the general public, and in industry, agriculture, commerce, and other fields.

A key element in the British conversion program has been education. Beginning in the primary schools, the metric system is the only system of measurements taught. The general public is being educated into the metric language by means of newspapers, magazines, posters, radio, and television.

Additional methods have also been employed. A demonstration center was established where Britons could go to practice purchasing food, clothing, and other items using the metric system. The center proved highly popular and not a few Britons expressed surprise over the ease and convenience of using metric units. Many were also relieved that there were no serious problems regarding conversion from customary units to metric and vice versa.

Another device, made use of especially by British

manufacturers of packaged foods, was to keep the metric contents of packages close to the quantities used with the customary units of weights and measures. Thus, 125 grams was used as a fair approximation of ¼ pound; 250 grams for ½ pound; 500 grams for 1 pound; and 1 kilogram for 2 pounds. In this way purchasers did not feel completely at a loss about the quantities they were receiving.

England, almost ten years later, has about finished its conversion process. Surprising even the staunchest supporters of the metric system, the changeover has worked out with remarkable smoothness. None of the dire predictions made by the opponents of change — public confusion, chaos in industry, staggering cost — have developed.

With England's move in 1965, there now remains just one great power in the world that does not use the metric system for its official language of measurements, and that is the United States.

Earlier, we have seen how the United States, in a kind of stop-and-go manner, did at least approach the matter of whether or not to adopt the metric system of weights and measures. The two biggest advances occurred in 1866, when the metric system was first made legal in this country, and in 1893, when the redefined metric standards were made the nation's "fundamental standards" of length and mass (weight). But since then nearly all the moves toward accepting the metric language in this country have been made through nongovernment initiative. Many groups in industry, the medical profession, and science, appreciating the advantages offered by the metric system over customary units, have changed to metrics for their measurement needs.

One of the earliest and largest groups to make a change was the pharmaceutical industry, in the mid-1950s. Precise and uniform measurements are important elements in the manufacture of pharmaceutical products. A little too much or too little of some medicines can make a big difference. Before conversion, measurements were traditionally based on such units as ounces, grains, and minims. Now after two decades of using the much simpler and more efficient grams, milligrams, and cubic centimeters, among other metric measures, the pharmaceutical industry does not in the least regret having made the conversion.

The advantages, indeed, have been greater than anticipated. The manufacturing of drugs can be done with greater economy; it is easier to train personnel in the use of metric measurements; the chances of error have been greatly reduced; the list of specifications for thousands of complex drugs has been simplified.

People in fields related to the pharmaceutical industry, such as doctors, pharmacists, and members of hospital staffs, have joined in the use of the language of metrics. Doctors learn early in their training how to specify drug dosage in

The pharmaceutical industry in the United States converted to the metric system in the mid-1950s.

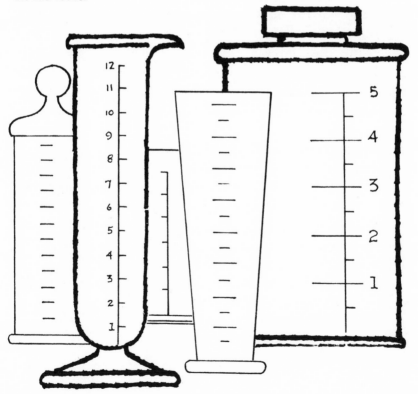

metric measurements and write their drug prescriptions in metric units. And of course, in order for these prescriptions to be properly filled, pharmacists must know metric measures also.

Other significant advances toward adoption of the metric system have been made in science. Scientists, as we know, have long been among the staunchest supporters of the exclusive use of metric measurements. In the United States today there is scarcely a field of scientific research that does not employ metric units for measurement purposes. There are also numerous branches of engineering where only metric measures are used.

In this last connection it is interesting and significant to note that many large American corporations with factories in foreign countries, or which depend heavily for their business on overseas markets, see to it that all their engineering drawings carry dimensions both in inches and metrics. Companies engaging in this practice have found it easier and less costly than the old way of converting customary units to metric measures in the countries using the metric system.

An equally important advance toward metric measurements in the United States is currently being made by the automotive industry. This conversion promises to be slow and long drawn out because of the huge number of automotive vehicles produced every year, and the hundreds of parts involved in each one.

The changeover is inevitable, however, since it will enable American car manufacturers better to meet the challenge of foreign competitors both here and abroad. Even now there are many cars coming off the assembly lines in Detroit with engines, transmissions, and other parts made to metric specifications.

And since thousands of foreign-built cars are already rolling along highways in the United States, auto mechanics are finding it increasingly necessary to equip themselves with tools made to metric standards.

Another inroad on the automotive world by the metric system has to do with the current major problem of air pollution. Automobile emissions of hydrocarbons are rated on the basis of metric standards as grams per mile traveled, for example, thereby combining two measurement systems.

In spite of general government apathy, certain agencies of the federal government have also found it advantageous to use the metric system instead of customary units. For a good number of years now, the United States Army has been employing metric measurements for designating various sizes of fighting equipment and ammunition. The 155-millimeter (155-mm) cannon, for example, indicates the size of the bore by its name. The army's use of metric measurements also helps to coordinate this nation's defense equipment with that of other countries.

The United States Coast and Geodetic Survey uses metric measurements, as does the National Bureau of Standards. In 1963 the latter adopted the international metric system for use in all research work and in the preparation of its numerous publications. The only exception is where metrics would interfere with the effectiveness of exchanging information with groups not familiar with metric measurements.

The National Aeronautics and Space Administration, engaged in some of the most exciting technical accomplishments of this century, including the landing of men on the moon, adopted the metric system in 1971 for its activities. Technical data in the formal reports published by NASA are expressed in metric terms. There are highway signs in Ohio that indicate mileage in both kilometers and miles.

Numerous other examples of the conversion to metric measurements in the United States could be cited. Even though the system's most enthusiastic supporters may feel that changeover is painfully slow, it is evident that it is taking place at a steady rate. This development can have only one result: the United States will in the near future become a member of the world family of metric users.

The United States must adopt the metric system if for no other reason than that which made England change: to be able to compete in world markets on equal terms with the metric-using nations. The cost of achieving this changeover can be great. But the economic loss due to an inability to sell products overseas is probably even greater.

There is another important aspect to this question of international trade. Many manufactured products have interchangeable parts, each made to certain fixed standards. Examples are nut and bolt sizes, wire thicknesses, and dimensions of various steel products and the thousands of items used in the electronics industry. This interchangeability makes for ease of mass production, as well as of repair and maintenance.

Recently there has been increased activity on behalf of the establishment of international standards for all sorts of materials and products. These new international standards are to be based on metric measurements. Since the United States is not a metric country, at this writing, we could not only be left out of the discussions and decisions about such

In some states highway speed limit signs are beginning to appear with both metric and conventional information.

standards, but could be seriously handicapped in our ability to trade with other nations.

Of course, not everyone in this country is enthusiastically in favor of abandoning our customary units for the metric system. There are many antimetric individuals and groups who firmly believe in the customary units, citing the fact that these have served us well in attaining America's worldwide leadership in technology. A change to metric, they feel, could only bring extreme confusion to our industrial and economic life and to the public at large. However, at this point in the pro and con of the subject, it would appear that the forces against metric are backing a lost cause.

In 1971 the National Bureau of Standards completed a three-year study of the metric system as it relates to the United States. In July of that year a report was submitted to Congress (which had authorized the study) entitled *A Metric America: A Decision Whose Time Has Come.* (See Bibliography.)

This was the latest of a number of such reports requested by the Congress over a period of almost two hundred years. Conceivably, it could be the last. The report presents a clear picture of the metric system, and its writers lean to a decision calling for the adoption of the metric system by the United States.

At the time the report was submitted, the secretary of commerce said: "For many years, this Nation has been slowly going metric, and it would continue to do so regardless of national plans and policies. At the same time the worldwide use of the metric system is increasing, and today ours is the only major nation which has not decided to take such a step. As the report states, a metric America would seem to be desirable in terms of our stake in world trade, the development of international standards, relations with our neighbors and other countries, and national security."

In 1972 the United States Congress very nearly did make this country's conversion to the metric system an official reality. The Senate passed a bill that would have made the metric units the only legal weights and measures language in the nation. The bill failed to pass in the House of Representatives, however, due mainly to the fact that Congress was in a rush to adjourn and the metric conversion bill, along with numerous others, simply never reached the floor of the House for a vote. Nevertheless, by the time these words are being read, another bill converting this country to metrics may have passed.

Assuming that the United States will one day in the near future change over to the metric system, how will the conversion be achieved? We can follow the examples of other nations which have accomplished the task. One of the most recent and probably the most suitable for us would be that of England. Our two countries have much in common with respect to language, the system of weights and measures used (before England went metric), and economy.

In all probability the changeover will be accomplished within ten years at a gradual pace, since a crash program would assuredly produce chaos. Conversion to metric may take place in one segment of our society at a time, a kind of step-by-step process. Thus, for example, the steel industry can convert at one period, then the lumber industry several months later, and so on.

One of the chief factors assuring the success of the conversion program will be education. This can begin in the primary schools, where the metric system would be the only measurement language taught. In schools in California and Maine metric measures are already being taught along with the customary units.

Those of us who have dealt with nothing but customary units all our lives will not be neglected in the educational phase of the conversion program. As in England, our training in metrics will be helped by newspaper instructions, magazine articles, posters on billboards, in subways and on buses, and, of course, by the use of radio and television.

Mass communication, developed in the United States to an extremely fine art, can make metric users of us all in a reasonably short time.

A federally appointed commission of experts in the measurement field, as well as other experts, will direct the conversion program, ironing out difficulties wherever they crop up and seeing to it generally that the changeover takes place progressively and according to a prescribed schedule.

Other nations in the world have succeeded in changing their conventional measurement language to the metric system without serious difficulties. There appears to be no reason why the United States cannot do the same.

Many schools in the United States already are teaching metric weights and measures to students.

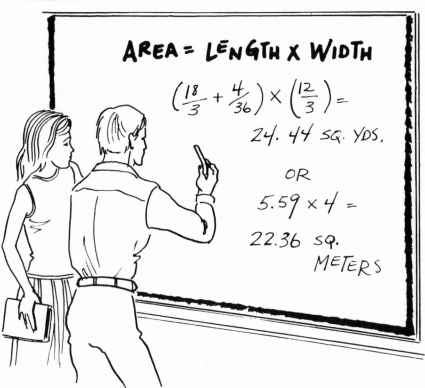

Appendix 1

Some Useful Metric Tables and Conversion Charts: Names
and Symbols for Metric Prefixes That May Be Applied to All
SI Units

MULTIPLE AND SUBMULTIPLE	PREFIX	SYMBOL	MEANING
$1\ 000\ 000\ 000\ 000 = 10^{12}$	tera (ter'a)	T	one trillion times
$1\ 000\ 000\ 000 = 10^{9}$	giga (ji'ga)	G	one billion times
$1\ 000\ 000 = 10^{6}$	mega (meg'a)	M*	one million times
$1\ 000 = 10^{3}$	kilo (kil'o)	k*	one thousand times
$100 = 10^{2}$	hecto (hek'to)	h	one hundred times
$10 = 10$	deka (dek'a)	da	ten times
$0.1 = 10^{-1}$	deci (des'i)	d	one-tenth of
$0.01 = 10^{-2}$	centi (sen'ti)	c*	one-hundredth of
$0.001 = 10^{-3}$	milli (mil'i)	m*	one-thousandth of
$0.000\ 001 = 10^{-6}$	micro (mi'kro)	μ*	one-millionth of
$0.000\ 000\ 001 = 10^{-9}$	nano (nan'o)	n	one-billionth of
$0.000\ 000\ 000\ 001 = 10^{-12}$	pico (pe'ko)	p	one-trillionth of
$0.000\ 000\ 000\ 000\ 001 = 10^{-15}$	femto (fem'to)	f	one-quadrillionth of
$0.000\ 000\ 000\ 000\ 000\ 001 = 10^{-18}$	atto (at'to)	a	one-quintillionth of

* Most commonly used.

112

Appendix 2

Metric Units and Their Relationship to One Another*

	UNIT	SYMBOL	RELATIONSHIP OF UNITS

Length

UNIT	SYMBOL	RELATIONSHIP OF UNITS
millimeter	mm	1 mm = 0.001 m
centimeter	cm	1 cm = 10 mm
decimeter	dm	1 dm = 10 cm
meter	m	1 m = 100 cm
kilometer	km	1 km = 1000 m

Area

UNIT	SYMBOL	RELATIONSHIP OF UNITS
square centimeter	cm²	1 cm² = 100 mm²
square decimeter	dm²	1 dm² = 100 cm²
square meter	m²	1 m² = 100 dm²
are	a	1 a = 100 m²
hectare	ha	1 ha = 100 a
square kilometer	km²	1 km² = 100 ha

Volume

UNIT	SYMBOL	RELATIONSHIP OF UNITS
cubic centimeter	cm³	
or milliliter	ml	$\left.\begin{array}{l} 1\ cm^3 \\ 1\ ml \end{array}\right\} = 0.001\ l$
cubic decimeter	dm³	
or liter	l	$\left.\begin{array}{l} 1\ dm^3 \\ 1\ l \end{array}\right\} = 1{,}000\ ml$
cubic meter	m³	1 m³ = 1,000 l

Mass

UNIT	SYMBOL	RELATIONSHIP OF UNITS
milligram	mg	1 mg = 0.001 g
gram	g	1 g = 1,000 mg
kilogram	kg	1 kg = 1,000 g
metric ton	t	1 t = 1,000 kg

* From Metric Association, Inc., *Metric Units of Measure* (see Bibliography).

Appendix 3

Approximate Common Equivalents: Metric to U.S. Customary Units

Length

1 millimeter (mm)	=	0.04 inch
1 centimeter (cm)	=	0.4 inch
1 meter (m)	=	3.3 feet
	=	1.1 yards
1 kilometer (km)	=	0.6 mile

Area

1 square centimeter (cm²)	=	0.16 square inch
1 square meter (m²)	=	11.0 square feet
	=	1.2 square yards
1 hectare (ha)	=	2.5 acres
1 square kilometer (km²)	=	0.39 square mile

Mass

1 milligram (mg)	=	0.015 grain
1 gram (g)	=	0.035 ounce
1 kilogram (kg)	=	2.2 pounds
1 metric ton	=	1.102 tons (short)

Volume

1 cubic centimeter (cm³)	=	0.06 cubic inch
1 cubic meter (m³)	=	35.0 cubic feet
	=	1.3 cubic yards
1 milliliter (ml)	=	0.2 teaspoon
	=	0.07 tablespoon
	=	0.03 fluid ounce
1 liter (l)	=	4.2 cups
	=	2.1 pints
	=	1.1 quarts
1 cubic meter (m³)	=	264.0 gallons
	=	113.0 pecks
	=	28.0 bushels

Appendix 4

Approximate Common Equivalents: U.S. to Metric

Length

1 inch	= 25.0 millimeters (mm)
1 foot	= 0.3 meter (m)
1 yard	= 0.9 meter (m)
1 mile	= 1.6 kilometers (km)

Area

1 square inch	=	6.5 square centimeters (cm²)
1 square foot	=	0.09 square meter (m²)
1 square yard	=	0.8 square meter (m²)
1 acre	=	0.4 hectare (ha)*
1 square mile	=	2.6 square kilometers (km²)

Mass

1 grain	= 64.8 milligrams (mg)
1 ounce (dry)	= 28.3 grams (g)
1 pound	= 0.45 kilogram (kg)
1 short ton	= 0.907 metric tons

Volume

1 cubic inch	= 16.0 cubic centimeters (cm³)
1 cubic foot	= 0.03 cubic meter (m³)
1 cubic yard	= 0.76 cubic meter (m³)
1 teaspoon	= 5.0 milliliters (ml)
1 tablespoon	= 15.0 milliliters (ml)
1 fluid ounce	= 30.0 milliliters (ml)
1 cup	= 0.24 liter (l)†

Volume (continued)

1 pint	=	0.47 liter (l)
1 quart	=	0.95 liter (l)
1 gallon	=	0.004 cubic meter (m³)
1 peck	=	0.009 cubic meter (m³)
1 bushel	=	0.04 cubic meter (m³)

Power

1 horsepower = 0.75 kilowatt (kw)

Energy

1 calorie = 4.18 joules (j)

* 1 hectare equals 10,000 square meters.

† In 1964 the twelfth General Conference on Weights and Measures redefined the liter as equal to 1 cubic decimeter (dm³). Previously, the liter was the volume of 1 kilogram of pure water at 4 degrees Celsius (centigrade). This is slightly larger than a cubic decimeter.

Appendix 5

Approximate Conversions from Customary to Metric and
Vice Versa*

WHEN YOU KNOW	YOU CAN FIND	IF YOU MULTIPLY BY
Length		
inches	millimeters	25
feet	centimeters	30
yards	meters	0.9
miles	kilometers	1.6
millimeters	inches	0.04
centimeters	inches	0.4
meters	yards	1.1
kilometers	miles	0.6
Area		
square inches	square centimeters	6.5
square feet	square meters	0.09
square yards	square meters	0.8
square miles	square kilometers	2.6
acres	square hectometers (hectares)	0.4
square centimeters	square inches	0.16
square meters	square yards	1.2
square kilometers	square miles	0.4
square hectometers (hectares)	acres	2.5

WHEN YOU KNOW	YOU CAN FIND	IF YOU MULTIPLY BY
Mass		
ounces	grams	28
pounds	kilograms	0.45
short tons	megagrams (metric tons)	0.9
grams	ounces	0.035
kilograms	pounds	2.2
megagrams (metric tons)	short tons	1.1
Volume		
ounces	milliliters	30
pints	liters	0.47
quarts	liters	0.95
gallons	liters	3.8
milliliters	ounces	0.034
liters	pints	2.1
liters	quarts	1.06
liters	gallons	0.26
Temperature		
degrees Fahrenheit	degrees Celsius	5/9 (after subtracting 32)
degrees Celsius	degrees Fahrenheit	9/5 (then add 32)

* From National Bureau of Standards, *A Metric America: A Decision Whose Time Has Come* (see Bibliography).

Appendix 6

Some Useful General Information on Metric Units

Length   The common metric units of length are the millimeter (mm) for small dimensions; the centimeter (cm) for ordinary practical use; the meter (m) for indicating dimensions of larger objects and short distances; and the kilometer (km) for longer distances. The centimeter is about 0.4 inch, the meter is about 40 inches, and the kilometer about 0.6 mile.

Area   Small areas are usually measured in square centimeters (cm²). The square meter (m²) is used for building and construction work and is about 20 percent larger than a square yard. The hectare is employed for land surveys and is equivalent to about 2.5 acres.

Volume   The most convenient metric unit for volume is the cubic decimeter (dm³), more commonly referred to as the liter (l). The liter is slightly larger than the U.S. liquid quart but smaller than the U.S. dry quart. In pharmacy and scientific work, the cubic centimeter (cm³), or milliliter (ml) as it is also called, is preferred. Where greater quantities are involved, as in the mixing of concrete and excavation work, the cubic meter (m³) is used.

Mass   In pharmaceutical and scientific work, the gram (g) is the most convenient metric unit. There are slightly less than 30 grams in one avoirdupois ounce. For most other uses the kilogram (kg) is convenient and is equivalent to about 2.2 pounds. The metric ton (t), 1,000 kilograms, is used for farm commodities, minerals, and other large quantities.

Temperature   All countries using the metric system of weights and measures also use the Celsius (°C, at one time called centigrade) scale for ordinary measurement of temperature. On the Celsius scale pure water at standard atmospheric pressure freezes at 0° and boils at 100°. In engineering and scientific work the kelvin (K) temperature scale is preferred. This has the same units as the Celsius (but on the Kelvin scale the freezing point of pure water is 273.16 K. Note that this is read "273.16 kelvins," not "273.16 degrees Kelvin").

* Based largely on Metric Association, Inc., *Metric Units of Measure* (see Bibliography).

Glossary

Aegina stater. Ancient Greek measure for weights and coinage.

American Metrological Society. A nineteenth-century group organized to promote the adoption of the metric system in the United States.

ampere. A basic unit in the metric system for the measurement of electric current.

amphora. A Roman unit of weight; also a pottery container used by the Greeks and Romans for shipping wine and olive oil.

are. Metric measure of land area equal to a square each of whose sides are 10 meters long.

Assize of Bread and Ale. Medieval English laws regulating the weight and prices of these commodities.

Attic foot. Ancient Greek measure equivalent to 12.1375 inches in our system of measurements.

avoirdupois. A medieval French term meaning "goods of weight." More commonly a pound measure equal to 16 ounces.

beam spectrometer. A laboratory tool used for recording the rate of speed of moving atoms.

bequa. An ancient Egyptian unit of weight measurement.

cable length. A mariners' measure of several values. One is the equivalent of 600 feet.

candela. A basic unit in the metric system for the measurement of luminous (light) intensity.

carat. A weight unit based on the carob seed and derived from the Arabs.

Celsius scale. A thermometer used with the metric system. It was invented by Anders Celsius, a Swedish astronomer. Sometimes called "centigrade scale." On the Celsius scale water freezes at 0 degrees and boils at 100 degrees.

commercial pound. An old English weight unit of about 15 ounces.

congius. An ancient Roman volume measure.

cubit. An ancient measure of length, from the elbow to the tip of the middle finger.

customary units. The name often used to designate the system of weights and measures used in the United States.

decimal. A system of numbers based on 10.

derived units. Secondary units of the metric system derived from the seven base units.

digit. An ancient unit of measure based on the width of the finger.

displacement ton. A maritime measurement term related to the weight of a ship empty of cargo.

drachma. An ancient Greek unit of measure for weights and coinage.

dram. Apothecaries' unit of weight equal to 1/8 ounce.

Drusian foot. An old Anglo-Saxon measure of length, about 13.2 inches.

electromagnetic field. A field of force made up of associated electrical and magnetic components.

ell. An ancient unit of length measuring from the tip of the middle finger, with arm fully extended at the side, to the nose. It was roughly equivalent to 3 feet.

English water ton. A unit of weight equal to 224 British imperial gallons.

ephemeris time. A measurement of time related to the earth's speed of rotation.

Fahrenheit scale. Our customary scale in the U.S. On the Fahrenheit scale water freezes at 32 degrees and boils at 212 degrees.

fathom. A measure of length equal to 6 feet. It is used by seamen in measuring the depth of water.

freight ton. A weight unit equal to 40 cubic feet. It is used to measure cargo.

furlong. An old Anglo-Saxon term meaning "furrow-long." As a unit of length measurement it is equal to 660 feet. Eight furlongs make 1 mile.

geodetic survey. An activity that deals with precise measurements of the earth's surface.

gin. An ancient Sumerian unit of measure equal to the square of a cubit.

gird. An old Anglo-Saxon measure for the yard.

great span. An ancient method for measuring length. It was equal to the distance between the thumb and little finger with hand outspread.

hertz. One of the derived units of the metric system. It is related to the physical quantity of frequency (cycles per second) in the field of electromagnetics. The unit is named for Heinrich Rudolph Hertz, a German physicist.

hogshead. An old English unit for weighing quantities of ale and beer.

hundredweight. A quantity measure equal to 100 pounds.

iugerum. An ancient Roman measure for area. It was equal to 28,800 square Roman feet.

International Institute for Preserving and Perfecting Weights and Measures. A nineteenth-century group formed in the United States for keeping the customary system of weights and measures.

joule. A derived unit of the metric system designating physical quantity of energy. It is named for James Prescott Joule, a British physicist.

kelvin. One of the seven basic units of the modern metric system. It is used as a basic measure (equivalent to a degree) for temperature. The unit is named for the English physicist William Thompson (Lord Kelvin).

Kelvin scale. This scale and the Celsius scale are both used with the metric system. On the Kelvin scale the coldest possible temperature (absolute zero) is 0 kelvins. Water freezes at 273.16 kelvins and boils at 375.15 kelvins.

khet. A basic square unit in the ancient Egyptian system of measurements. It had 100 royal cubits on a side.

latitude. A series of imaginary lines parallel to, and north and south of, the equator. Latitude is used along with longitude in a method for determining precisely points on the earth's surface.

libra. An old Roman term for the pound unit of measure.

little span. An ancient method for measuring short lengths. It was equal to the distance between the tips of the thumb and index finger spread wide.

longitude. A series of imaginary lines running around the earth through the north and south poles. See LATITUDE.

long ton. In the British imperial system of measures this was a weight equal to 2,240 pounds.

Magna Carta (Great Charter). A document signed by King John at Runnymede in 1215 that gave a measure of human freedom to Englishmen.

mass. The physical quantity of a substance.

meridian. An imaginary circle on the surface of the earth at any given place and passing through the north and south poles.

metric ton. A volume measure in the metric system equal to 1,000 kilograms, or about 2,205 pounds.

metrologists. Experts in the field of weights and measures.

metrology. The science of weights and measures.

milia passuum. A "thousand paces" in Latin and the basis of the old Roman mile.

mina. A Sumerian sexagesimal unit of weight.

minims. A unit of apothecary weight equal to 1/60 dram.

modius. A Roman basic unit for measuring the volume of dry substances such as corn, wheat, and lentils.

mole. One of the seven basic units in the modern metric system. It designates the amount of a substance.

nautical mile. A mile used by mariners. Equal to 6,076.1 feet.

newton. One of the derived units of the modern metric system. It is the unit of force. It is named for Isaac Newton, a famous British physicist.

ohm. This is another in the large family of derived units in the modern metric system. It represents the physical quantity of electrical resistance.

palm. An ancient measure based on the width of the hand. It was roughly 4 inches in length.

pes. The Roman word for "foot." The pes was a unit of length of 11.654 inches in our system of measurements.

pipe. An old English unit of measurement. It was used for doling out quantities of whiskey and beer.

quadrant. A fourth part of a circle.

radian. One of the two supplementary units in the modern metric system. It designates the measure of a plane angle.

register ton. A weight unit equal to 100 cubic feet. A measure of volume (not weight) used in the maritime field.

Roman foot. See PES.

second. One of the seven basic units in the modern metric system. It relates to time: the minute, hour, and (24-hour) day are derived from it.

sexagesimal. A numerical system based on the number 60.

sextarius. An ancient Roman liquid measure equal to a pint in our customary system of measures.

shekel. An early Sumerian sexagesimal unit of weight. Also used for coinage throughout the ancient Mediterranean world.

short ton. The customary or common American ton of 2,000 pounds.

SI. The official abbreviated designation for the modern metric system. It stands for Le *Système International* d'Unités (International System of Units).

stadion. An ancient Greek measure of about 600 feet in our system of measures. It is the origin of our word "stadium."

standards. Physical representations of units of measure.

steradian. One of two supplementary units in the modern metric system. It denotes the measure of a solid angle.

talent. An old Sumerian unit of weight equivalent to 60 minas. It was also used for coinage in early Mediterranean civilizations.

thermodynamic. Having to do, in physics, with the mechanical action of heat.

timber ton. A volume measure equal to 40 cubic feet.

ton. From the old Anglo-Saxon word *tun* given to a volume unit of measure for large quantities. In our system of measures the usual ton (short ton) is equal to 2,000 pounds.

tower pound. A popular weight unit of thirteenth-century England. It was equivalent to 12 ounces.

Treaty of the Meter. A treaty signed by seventeen nations in 1875, including the United States, for the purpose of refining and expanding the metric system.

triple point of water. The temperature at which water exists in three states: liquid, vapor, and solid (ice).

Troughton bar. A measurement standard for the English yard. It was brought to the United States in 1814 for use in geodetic survey work.

troy pound. A unit of weight of close to 13 ounces. Named after the French city of Troyes.

unciae. The twelfth part of the Roman foot measure. Our words "inch" and "ounce" are derived from *unciae*.

unit of measure. A particular value given a quantity of weight, capacity, length, or sometimes other quantities, in a system of measures.

volt. One of the derived units in the modern metric system. It represents electrical voltage (potential difference). The unit is named for Alessandro Volta, an Italian physicist.

volume. The amount of space occupied by a substance. It is measured in cubic values—cubic feet, cubic centimeters, and so on.

watt. A derived unit in the modern metric system. It represents the physical quantity of power. The unit is named for James Watt, an early English physicist.

weight. Corresponds to the force of gravity acting on a given substance (mass). Weight equals mass times acceleration of gravity.

wheat ton. A volume measure equal to 20 bushels of grain.

Winchester wine gallon. An English liquid measure of the Middle Ages. It still serves as the basis for the United States gallon.

For Additional Reading

BOOKS

Asimov, Isaac. *Realm of Measure*. Boston: Houghton Mifflin, 1960.

Donovan, Frank. *Prepare Now for a Metric Future.* New York: Weybright and Talley, 1970.

Ede, A. J. *Advantages of the Metric System.* London: Her Majesty's Stationery Office, 1972.

National Bureau of Standards. *A History of the Metric System Controversy in the United States.* Washington, D.C.: NBS Special Publication 345–10, 1971.

———. *A Metric America: A Decision Whose Time Has Come.* Washington, D.C.: NBS Special Publication 345, 1971.

The two books from the National Bureau of Standards may be purchased for $2.25 each from Superintendent of Documents, U.S. Government Printing Office, Washington, D.C. 20402.

MAGAZINE ARTICLES AND BOOKLETS

American Society for Testing and Materials. *Standard Metric Practice Guide (A Guide to the Use of SI–the International System of Units).* ASTM Pamphlet E380–70, 1970.

Edelson, Edward. "Here Comes the New Yardstick in Your Life." *Popular Science,* November 1973.

Ford Motor Co. (Engineering Staff). *Measuring Systems and Their History.* Dearborn, Mich.: 1966.

Lincoln, Marshall. "Going Metric Makes the Figuring Easier in Your Shop." *Popular Science,* November 1973.

Metric Association. *Metric Units of Measure.* 10th ed. 1972. (Available for 15¢ from Metric Association, Inc., 2004 Ash St., Waukegan, Ill. 60085.)

Perry, H. Allen. "Inching Towards the Metric System." *American Legion Magazine,* July 1972.

Ritchie-Calder, Lord. "Conversion to the Metric System." *Scientific American,* July 1970.

Index